Don't Blink!

Just suppose you never had read anything about African animals, never saw a picture, never heard of their existence—and one morning at 7 A.M. you looked out the window and saw twenty giraffes in a row feeding on the trees of your block. What would you think?

If you're like most people, you'd draw your shades, blink your eyes and try to forget about it. That's the way most people are when they encounter something they hadn't known existed and can't assimilate the experience.

That's also the way many people approach the spiritual world. We might have even experienced phenomena like an answered prayer—one of those odd coincidences that seems to be so much more than a coincidence—but it's easy to close the shades, blink our eyes and forget about it.

This book asks you not to close the shades but to look again. Don't blink. Stare. Gaze. Contemplate. Reality is its own reward, but there are many undiscovered realities and they go undiscovered because the meaning is threatening. Don't blink, but read on.

Moishe Rosen is the executive director of Jews for Jesus. This book is a presentation of his thoughts and understandings of Scripture. The Jews for Jesus organization has no official position on these issues because, like the rest of the body of Christ, it is comprised of many individuals who hold many different viewpoints regarding last things and end times.

This book reflects one man's thinking. His thinking does not carry the endorsement of the Jews for Jesus board of directors, staff or supporters.

Likewise, Campus Crusade for Christ International, owner of Here's Life Publishers, does not take an official position regarding the relationship between global events and biblical prophecy, and thus does not necessarily endorse the views expressed herein. The publisher presents *Overture to Armaggedon?* as one man's informed opinion — the perspective of a Jew who believes in Jesus on how world events may converge with biblical prophecy in the near future. Its sole intent is to encourage readers to consider the message of the Holy Scriptures and ask themselves, "How should we then live?"

Beyond the Gulf War

Overture to Armageddon?

MOISHE ROSEN
Founder, Jews for Jesus

with Bob Massie

Here's Life Publishers

First Printing, April 1991

Published by
HERE'S LIFE PUBLISHERS, INC.
P. O. Box 1576
San Bernardino, CA 92402

Unless indicated otherwise, Scripture quotations are from *The Holy Bible: New International Version,* © 1973, 1978, 1984 by the International Bible Society. Published by Zondervan Bible Publishers, Grand Rapids, Michigan.
Scripture quotations designated KJV are from the *King James Version.*

Cover design by Garborg Design Works
Background photography by M. Angelo/Westlight

For More Information, Write:
L.I.F.E.—P.O. Box A399, Sydney South 2000, Australia
Campus Crusade for Christ of Canada—Box 300, Vancouver, B.C., V6C 2X3, Canada
Campus Crusade for Christ—Pearl Assurance House, 4 Temple Row, Birmingham, B2 5HG, England
Lay Institute for Evangelism—P.O. Box 8786, Auckland 3, New Zealand
Campus Crusade for Christ—P.O. Box 240, Raffles City Post Office, Singapore 9117
Great Commission Movement of Nigeria—P.O. Box 500, Jos, Plateau State Nigeria, West Africa
Campus Crusade for Christ International—Arrowhead Springs, San Bernardino, CA 92414, U.S.A.

Contents

Note

B.C.E. stands for "before the common era" and is
equivalent to B.C. (before Christ). C.E. refers to the "common
era" and is the same as A.D. (*anno Domini*).

FOREWORD

Every now and then I get a phone call from my friend, Moishe Rosen, or we cross paths at some kind of gathering and catch up on each other. On the surface he always seems relaxed and laid back, but underneath, here is a giant of a man who is finely tuned, quick thinking, strongly focused and deeply committed to Jesus Christ.

I first met Moishe when he was Martin. Even the changing of his name indicates that the more he's been captured by Y'shua, his Messiah, the more intensely Jewish he's become. From the first time he entered my study we liked each other, and he soon lured me from study to delicatessens for lunches. Moishe knows every good Jewish deli from the Pacific Ocean inward throughout the whole Los Angeles basin; and he loves to park his great frame on an ice-cream-parlor chair in one of the crowded, noisy eating areas, hunch over a little round faux-marble-topped table, consume giant sandwiches and monstrous pickles, and amid pungent aromas and sweet-sour Yiddish music, talk politics, history, the arts, and most of all Y'shua.

My wife Anne and I have just read the manuscript of this book, and certainly it reflects Moishe's fine mind, grasp of history, comprehensive knowledge of the Bible, and great good common sense.

What a timely contribution! Fictional human characters play up our current times, especially as they spotlight the great social, political and even personality struggles of that boiling pot, the Middle East.

Thank you, Here's Life Publishers.

Thank you, collaborator Bob Massie.

Thank you, my friend Moishe Rosen. A warm embrace and a kiss on each cheek.

RAYMOND C. ORTLUND
Newport Beach, California

About This Book

All of us love a good story. Whether it's to be entertained, to be moved, or to be challenged, we love to read about other people and their lives.

And most of the time we walk away from stories with a new idea or two.

Like that famous storyteller, Jesus of Nazareth, Moishe Rosen and I like to tell stories to help people "put skin on" ideas. We've included a lot of both—stories and ideas—in this book. We think that by meeting characters, weighing new ideas, ruminating on "what if ?" and considering the claims of Scripture, you're in for a "good read" that might just change your life.

So whether you get into our stories about people who view current and future events in light of their own sense of spiritual reality, or the horizon-stretching predictions of ancient prophets that are as relevant as tomorrow's headlines, enjoy yourself. Think a lot. Question hard. Be open.

Be forewarned, and please don't be offended, that we present a few fairly graphic lifestyle descriptions in the early going. We assure you we have both encountered far greater extremes in real-life people; in fact, each of our fictional characters in the first four chapters are disguised composites drawn from several real people we know. We share these scenarios to illustrate the lengths to which our world will go to find spiritual reality in an uncertain future.

Oh, and don't start this book late in the evening if you like to go to bed at a decent hour. Like with those late night movies, you'll want to stay with *Overture to Armageddon?* until the fat lady sings.

BOB MASSIE

A Word From the Author . . .

A Little Child Shall Lead/Leave Them

My daughter, Ruth Rosen, is no longer "a little child." She is a grown lady with an education and outlook similar to my own. Furthermore, she is one of the more than 100 staff people of the Jews for Jesus ministry. She shares my concern that most people have never really heard about Y'shua (that's the Jewish way to say Jesus) in the way that it should be told. This is not to say that most people haven't heard of Jesus, but the way they've heard it didn't allow them to approach and see who and what He really is.

Conventional Christendom speaks in tones that could begin with a prologue, "Long ago, far away . . . " and then go on to tell about the two-dimensional Jesus who used to be, and how He loved children and how He loved the world. It's also easy to picture Him in some meadow like Ferdinand the Bull, enjoying His own gentleness and the reverie of a flower-filled world.

The problem of the presentation of Jesus is not that it's been either undertold or overtold, but rather that those who wanted to tell the story have often misrepresented the nature of the truth. Several months ago, Ruth came to me and told what she felt was part of the problem. People who didn't believe in Y'shua needed more of a vantage point of who He is in the future and the here and now and how He ties in with world history. Then when things began happening in the land that in ancient times was called Babylon, and when it became more than ancient history, and the prophecies seemed so relevant, I thought this to be a good time to write and tell you about the modern-times Y'shua and what He wants from you.

MOISHE ROSEN

A WARNING TO THE READER

The first few chapters of this book contain graphic descriptions that some might find disturbing. It is intended to shock the reader, but only because the realities of life are often shocking. The characters you meet in the early chapters of this book are not "real," but they could be. They are composites of various people I have met in the course of ministry over the years.

MOISHE ROSEN

*The weak, the defenseless—how he
loved to hate them.*

---

1. LORD OF THE DARKNESS

Sam Trevanti glided into the teachers' lounge at Merit High School with the relaxed air of a confident athlete. Mrs. Presley was at the soft-drink machine, feeding it nickels and waiting for the Coke Classic to drop. Everything else in the machine was diet-this or diet-that, but the principal keeps Coke Classic on hand because Mrs. Presley is a squeaky wheel.

"Hello, Mrs. Presley." Sam smiled pleasantly as he passed her on his way to the time-softened leather couch. *Burn in hell, you stupid old bat,* he silently added as he sank down into the cracked cushions and lost himself in the newspaper's latest reports of troop withdrawals from the Persian Gulf.

Sam was disappointed in the way the Iraqi thing had played out. No, more like frustrated. He thought Saddam Hussein had a good thing going until he made the stupid mistake of invading Kuwait and getting the rest of the world involved.

If he'd just kept a low profile . . .

Sam Trevanti is 32 years old, Merit High's gym teacher, basketball coach, and resident not-so-eligible bachelor. He never married because as a young adult, he found women a problem. It's not that they didn't like him. No, there were plenty of candidates for a guy as fastidious about his appearance and manners as Sam.

Sam found women a problem because he wasn't looking for someone to love. He was looking for someone to adore him. He didn't want a relationship; he wanted a devotee. He wanted a woman who craved him so completely that she would pour herself out before him, a woman who would prove her devotion by embracing the pain he would inflict as a test.

What Sam really wanted was to humiliate women, to make them grovel in adoration before him. He proudly envisioned himself as having the sexual equipment and endurance of a satyr.

The only thing he found attractive or appealing about women was their vulnerablity. He desired to have them — their love and adoration — only if it was understood he would give nothing in return.

Nothing good, that is.

It was perverse. He knew that, but it didn't bother him. He was comfortable with who he was. What was there about conventional society that he should emulate?

The secret abuses he had endured so long ago, the ones forced on him by "conventional" figures, had confused and terrified him at first. But he had learned to adapt. Around his inner hatred of the people in his world he wrapped a carefully crafted and maintained exterior which was exemplary.

To please his mother he became an altar boy. To please himself he spat on the crucifix as he polished it in feigned devotion.

No one ever imagined the undercurrent of evil thoughts and quietly uttered obscenities that kept that well-behaved child smiling as he buffed the statue with the polishing cloth the old priest kept in the corner closet.

As a teenager, Sam decided to make up his own religion, one that would revolve around himself and the meeting of his own insatiable desires instead of the desires of others. He tried thinking of himself as the god of his religion; it seemed logical, but somehow it left him feeling a little empty because he had no worshippers.

So he constructed in his mind an image of a superior being, a being who like himself was never satisfied, who like himself wanted people to grovel before him, who like himself was strong enough not to submit to the conventionalities of those who were weaker-willed.

One night, when the house was quiet and the rest of the family asleep, Sam was surprised to find himself singing an ode to this being. It was not a song he had ever heard— just a simple tune with simple words that seemed to arise from a well somewhere deep within. In it, he expressed his adoration for the spirit of darkness which had always held such terror and comfort for him.

As he sang quietly he sensed a presence—a presence of darkness, different from the portiere of dusk that hung in his room after the lights were turned out. It's not that it was darker than the night or more terrible, but . . . .

It was alive.

At that moment, Sam realized he had not imagined a pretend being. His made-up religion was real. And so was his god, now his lord, Satan.

That night, he found himself—and this was all by himself—promising Satan that he would do something to show his contempt for the silly rules that were beneath him and his new-found lord.

It would be just a small act of destruction, but it would be in Satan's name.

A week later, the night before the trash man was to come, Sam crept out of his house in the middle of the night. Quietly he slashed and dumped all the trash bags, including his own, that lined his street. As the sun rose and the wind began to blow, the neighborhood began to look and smell like a garbage dump. Sam reveled in it! When his father expressed distress, he mimicked the shocked response and offered to help clean up the mess. But even as he worked, he made up a litany praising "Lord Satan who has the power to inflict distress."

Over the years, he engaged in acts that might be considered malicious mischief. He was careful not to go too far in any of them, and to minimize the possibility of detection. Yet with each act he committed, he thrilled to the knowledge that he was pleasing the one who is the source of all evil.

And the scale of his activity escalated.

Into adulthood.

By then he had devised other ways of wallowing in the evil he adored. He felt fulfilled each time he shocked or scared or dirtied those whom he considered weaker and less worthy than himself. He found special satisfaction in doing that which defied what others considered right.

Sam's mischief advanced to malevolence one night when he found a homeless drunk unconscious in the gutter. Realizing that the man was at his mercy, Sam sprinted home, grabbed the rose pruning shears from his father's shed and returned to the insensate man.

Weak, defenseless—how he loved to hate them.

Taking the drunk's right hand as tenderly as he would a lover's, he caressed the little finger, then severed it from its hand at the second joint.

He smiled, wishing the man hadn't anesthetized himself.

Back in his own apartment, Sam carefully constructed an altar and with reverence, offered the mutilated finger on it. He had reached what he felt was a high point in his life; yet it echoed with emptiness because he had no one with whom to share the ecstasy.

Years passed and Sam continued covertly, under his facade of conventionality, to wreak havoc on the conventional society he hated so. Yet he longed for camaraderie and the admiration of like-minded souls for his corruption. That longing ultimately led him to seek out a nearby Satanist church and attend one of the services.

It was a poorly done "black mass." The Satanist priest was largely a showman, and his litany to evil was no more powerful than the magic incantations of a circus performer. It might have satisfied a neophyte, but Sam sensed only a shadow of the reality he had known from the time when, as a boy, he had defiled the altar at Saint Barnabas Church.

He concluded, with disgust, that there was no more for him at a Satanist church than at a conventional church.

But he did sign his name on the guest register. He smirked as he realized that it was the same kind they had used in the parish of his childhood.

The call that came that evening still surprised him. It was one of the younger members who had noticed Sam at the mass. He insisted that he must be allowed to visit Sam in his apartment that very evening.

Reluctantly, Sam agreed. If the so-called Satanist had nothing more to offer than what he had seen at the church, he could always hide behind the pleasant face he wore in public.

He opened his door in response to the knock, and the young man who came in immediately dropped to his knees, prostrated himself and cried out, "Master! Teach me." Sam was stunned! With exulting and tearful joy the young man sobbed that he had recognized Sam as one of the faithful and only wanted to adore him and learn to be like him.

He began to kiss Sam's feet and offer himself to Sam in ways that Sam had always felt a woman should!

At that moment Sam had another revelation: gender didn't matter. It was not a sexual thing. It was the power over a properly submitted human being that brought him to an orgiastic emotional climax.

As the evening wore on, the two discussed what deliciously evil acts and manipulations might gratify them. Sam decided that all they would do for the moment would be to take an ice pick and puncture holes in the tires of all the ambulances at General Hospital. They laughed all the way back to Sam's home, gleeful as they envisioned a sufferer, waiting for an ambulance that could not come.

And they got drunk. That night, Sam discovered his true sexual identity. He was lifted to new heights as he realized that even as he was sexually devouring his partner they were both being exquisitely devoured by an unseen third partner.

As the weeks passed, the two continued to indulge in petty criminal acts, but the thrill was waning. What lasting pleasure could possibly come from spoiling what was already spoiled—drunks and hardened prostitutes?

To spoil the unspoiled—that would please the lord of darkness!

The planning would take months. It would require the most precise possible implementation.

But they would do it. They would go to extraordinary lengths to ensure success, and they would do it. They would kidnap, sacrifice, and eat — a child!

*   *   *

"Are you all right, Mr. Trevanti?" Mrs. Presley's nasal whine ripped Sam out of his reverie. There was no concern in her voice. Just her big, busy-body nose.

"Huh?" Sam grunted as his thoughts lurched from daydreaming about "The Plan" to the voice in the teachers' lounge. "Oh, yes. Yes, Mrs. Presley." He began to sit up. "I'm fine. Must have dozed off, thanks. I've just been having trouble sleeping lately — a lot on my mind."

"A guilty conscience? Naughty, naughty boy!"

Sam just smiled.

I wonder, *he thought,* if Saddam Hussein
was one of my kind?

---

2. THE WAY
OF THE WORLD

Sam Trevanti's head was buried in the local newspaper when Tessie Ginsberg and Roger Stanley entered the
teachers' lounge, laughing. " . . . and when she left the
room for the principal's office, the look she gave me could
have been grounds for arrest," Roger said.

"What would the charge have been?" Tessie quipped.

"Oh, murder. Definitely murder!"

"Hello, Sam." Tessie said to the gym teacher as she
eyed the paper. "Are more of our boys on their way home
from the Gulf?"

Sam didn't answer, so Tessie just shrugged her
shoulders and joined Roger at the snack machine.

If you were to open this particular vending machine
and look at the expiration dates on the packages, you'd
read, "Best if used before October 1989"; or, "2/2/90." A
wave of concern for overall health had washed over the staff
at Merit High School, causing them to abandon potato chips
in favor of the granola bars that were habitually under-
stocked.

"Damn!" Roger muttered as his eye landed on the empty slot where he expected to find his favorite snack.

"I got the last one." Sam held up the empty wrapper, crumpled it and let it drop to the cushion next to him. "But they're scheduled to restock the thing today."

"Oh, great. Terrific. So I get to play the Jew in the desert, waiting for the miraculous manna to appear."

A tinge of pain stabbed Tessie deep inside as Roger laughed at his attempted joke. Her lips pulled back in a grimace as she thought, *Father was right, may he rest in peace. Things never change.*

Tessie Ginsberg is Jewish, a widow now. Her husband of thirty-seven years died of cancer thirteen very long months ago. She didn't think her loneliness could get any worse, but when insensitive goyim like Roger made their remarks, it managed to make her feel even more alone. It reminded her that she is a widow, a Jewish widow, making her way in a Gentile world.

She wonders if anything in life will ever be good again. In fact, the sorrow and confusion she felt following the death of her dear David were such a burden that a few weeks after the funeral Tessie felt she had to do something about it just to keep her sanity.

It was something that to this day she fears her children will discover. Not a bad thing at all. She's just afraid that they wouldn't understand and that they would make her feel shame on top of her sorrow.

It happened about six weeks after she was widowed. David had always taken care of all their affairs—the checkbook, the credit cards, the safety deposit box, the insurance. He died so suddenly that he hadn't made provision for Tessie to take control of their finances, so she found herself in a very difficult situation. The safety deposit box was locked, and who knew where David's key was? None of the credit cards were in her name. The checking assets were frozen.

The house was in her name, thank God. But the banker had manipulated her into taking out a new mortgage so she would have money to get by. She didn't know how to calculate the loan, so what amounted to a 22 percent compound interest rate seemed as good as any.

When Tessie went to make the first payment on the new loan, the banker called her into his office. "Mrs. Ginsberg, you know that house is too much for you now that Mr. Ginsberg has," he paused respectfully, "passed on. Why don't you allow me to arrange for a realtor to sell it? Wouldn't you really be happier in a nice, cozy apartment?"

And they think we wheel and deal people for money! Tessie thought angrily. That was her home — hers and David's and the children's — and she was not going to sell it to strangers. But she was so confused.

Tessie didn't know where to turn for help. It certainly wouldn't be to the bankers and their ilk.

One gloomy evening she found herself thumbing through the yellow pages of the phone book, looking for something, anything, that might suggest itself as a way to help her sort through the confusion.

And there it was: Spiritual Advisor.

Now if it was spiritual help she needed, you would think she'd go to a rabbi. In fact, that's exactly what Tessie told herself as the advertisement caught her eye. But the rabbi she and David had known since they were married had moved to be closer to his children in California, and the new rabbi was awfully young.

Though she never would have complained, she really didn't like the way the new rabbi had conducted David's service. Oh, she couldn't blame him for not knowing all the wonderful things that she knew about David. And she knew she had been too distraught to make suggestions before the service. But it just wasn't right.

And, if the truth really were known, she was not entirely satisfied with the teaching of her temple on the afterlife. The rabbi had said, "Do good works and you will live on in the memory of your loved ones."

That had bothered her. Tessie had no problem with the importance of good works. She could appreciate that a person who was charitable and caring would be remembered, and that in a sense that was "living on."

But she thought a lot of it was word games. So much of what makes a person human is something you can't touch or see even under a microscope. What happens to a person after they die? Where does the part of you go which is transported by listening to a symphony? Does the love of a lifetime just disappear when the body stops functioning? How can a soul die, anyway? You can't touch it so it can't just decompose. Where does it go?

In her younger years she had asked her rabbi such questions. He had smiled at her warmly. "Tessie, I don't know and I'm not going to do you a disservice by pretending I do. In my opinion, we have a certain amount of time and that is it. Life is precious and we must use it as best we can, while we can. What happens when we die is uncertain. Though I don't believe in an afterlife, I cannot say for certain there is none. But with a beautiful soul like yours, I wouldn't worry."

In her youth, these words comforted her. As a widow in late middle-age, they were far from comforting.

That's why she contemplated seeing the spiritual advisor. She knew some Jews were very much into mysticism, and though she and her family were not, at least there was a precedent that made her feel it wasn't too "un-Jewish."

Tessie called on the phone and nervously asked the spiritual advisor about her training. The woman on the other end told her that she was an ordained minister in the Church of the Universe, a title granted after a rigorous course of study and the approval of the authorities over her.

Tessie thought that sounded all right, so she made an appointment and went to see her.

The woman who met Tessie at the door of the office was not wearing a clergy robe, nor was she wearing an exotic Gypsy outfit (Tessie had had her doubts). Instead, it was quite the opposite. She had on a smart business suit, shook Tessie's hand briskly, introduced herself as the Reverend Dr. Collins and escorted Tessie into a tastefully decorated office.

Tessie told her story as Dr. Collins nodded sympathetically and took notes on everything she said. That impressed her. No adult had ever taken notes on what she said before. After a full ninety minutes of questions and answers, tears and laughter, Tessie felt purged. She finally had been able to pour out all her grief and confusion.

Dr. Collins, obviously not done with the session, had said gently, "Tess, I know you feel better inside, but that feeling hasn't changed your situation. I want to help you with that, too. Now there is a long way and there is a short way. I'm a little hesitant to suggest the short way because I don't want you to misunderstand.

"My work is based on conclusive research, but I'm afraid that some of my more traditional colleagues look askance at some of my methods. The truth is, what I am doing actually pre-dates the bureaucratic system with all its red tape."

Tessie liked Dr. Collins, and she liked the idea of cutting through the bureaucratic mish-mosh. "So let them look askance; they are probably jealous. I'd like to hear what you have to say."

Dr. Collins proceeded to tell Tessie that according to recent research, crystals have certain inherent properties which can be helpful to people on many levels. She explained that crystals were being used in various applications, and that in those applications many were discovering new principles — principles which demonstrate that certain wave lengths had been absorbed into those crystals from people, from objects and from the whole of creation.

Tessie was a bit skeptical, but Dr. Collins had helped her thus far, so she listened.

"Tess, why don't you come with me." Dr. Collins led her into a study. Tessie was impressed by the thick pile carpet, the beautiful wood-paneled walls and the globe in the far corner. And the books! They stretched from the floor to the ceiling. There were so many that there was even a library ladder.

Dr. Collins invited Tessie to sit at a round table in the center of the room. She dimmed the room lights and turned up a single, bright overhead lamp which directed its beam downward in a tight circle. The table's rich brocade covering seemed iridescent in the glow.

Dr. Collins took the covering off the table and turned on a switch concealed on the bottom side of the round tabletop. With the hum of a quiet motor, a round, clear globe about five inches in diameter emerged from the opening in the center of the table.

It was a crystal ball.

As Tessie stared at it, she could see beautiful colors. She turned her head this way and that, and it seemed like a kaleidoscope, with blues and yellows and greens cascading outward.

When Dr. Collins sat down across from her, Tessie could see Dr. Collins's face through the crystal ball as if it were on water, shimmering with the dancing of the colors. Her smile was reassuring.

"Mrs. Ginsberg." The new formality seemed somehow appropriate to Tessie, as did the breathy whisper in which it was spoken. "Can you see me? Can you see the aura about me?"

Tessie was sure she could. She really could. There was something there. It was yellowish. It was out toward the edge of the globe, almost like a rainbow. She really could see the aura. "Yes," she murmured.

"And I can see and analyze the aura about you." Dr. Collins paused. "Oh, what a beautiful soul!" she said in a slow, reverent tone. "So calm. So quiet.

"But there's laughter." Dr. Collins raised her eyes to meet Tessie's and said, "I can tell there's been a lot of laughter in your life." Tessie smiled as the flood of memories began to bathe her eyes in tears.

Dr. Collins looked back to the crystal. "I also hear some sobs and some sorrow. Children's feet. A reassuring voice. 'Mom . . .'?

"And I see those problems. The endless column of numbers that won't add up. The confusion brought on by the different voices giving advice. The pain that still cuts through you like cold steel because of your loss."

Abruptly, Dr. Collins sat up. Once again she was brisk and businesslike. "Tess, I'd like to put you in touch with a financial advisor. I've seen enough to know that the best help I can give is to recommend a competent professional who will serve you well."

That was eleven months ago. Mr. Wilson from a brokerage house in the city had helped Tessie. He arranged for an attorney to settle the estate, helped her clear all debts, and advised her on how to invest her funds. Mr. Wilson was a man of integrity. He had handled things efficiently and without pressuring Tessie. It was wonderful. She knows that if she ever has another problem she can go back to Dr. Collins.

But she'd never tell her children.

* * *

Roger tapped the front of Sam's newspaper. "It's all the fault of the British," he announced as the paper collapsed in on Sam.

Sam fumbled with the paper then flicked it open again. "What are you talking about?" he asked, the boredom of his tone barely masked by the paper.

"This whole Middle East business," Roger said as he tapped the paper again, this time tapping just enough to point out the headline and the photo that occupied a good square foot of newsprint.

Roger teaches English at Merit High. He feels fortunate to have a job, what with the glut of English teachers on the market. His doctorate is in education, so the job market is even more limited for him. Someday he'd like to get a promotion to assistant principal or maybe work as a curriculum writer. He's a good writer.

Roger's father was a physician. He had absolutely no use for religion of any kind, though he didn't mind his family celebrating Christmas and other such holidays that were more for fun than anything else. Roger feels pretty much the same. If you asked what his religion was, he'd say, "I believe in history. I believe in things as they are. I don't know about a spirit world, and frankly, even if one exists, I don't see how anyone else can know either."

In college, Roger was influenced profoundly by a triumvirate of professors who were leading humanist writers. Two of them were involved in drafting the Humanist Manifesto.

He could trace the development of his worldview straight back to those three mentors. In his teen years, he had dabbled in religion of various kinds, wondering if there was any substance behind the forms, but each time he came up short. He was even mildly disappointed because others seemed to draw a degree of meaning and even intimacy from their religious experiences. He never found it.

The closest he came was in reading *Stages of Faith* by James Fowler. He could see that people go through different stages or plateaus of experience from which, when coupled with "faith," they discover a framework within which meaning in life can develop. That had made sense to him, but he wasn't sure which stage he was in or how to get on with the development to the next stage. He was sure it had to hold more meaning than the one he was in.

When he reached college, he saw the light. Religious experience only holds meaning for those who have limited, even naive concepts of the world and human society. What religions call spiritual reality in truth is the world of the abstract, the reality which the human mind, in all its vast powers, constructs *ex nihilo.*

He left the university with that reality neatly ordered and properly fitted for a lifetime of enlightening others.

But something happened that caused that world to be knocked a little off balance. Roger wouldn't tell you about it and he won't admit that it's had him wondering.

He doesn't know whether it was a dream, a trick of his imagination or what. It happened only three or four years ago, at the Community Center. Roger had joined because he knew that to advance in the field of education, you have to demonstrate your involvement in the lives of those around you.

It was autumn, the first semester of the school year, and the Center was sponsoring a haunted house to raise money. The members of the Center had gained permission to use a big, old, empty house on a street lined with big, old, droopy trees—perfect for their purpose.

They had worked for weeks, decorating and setting up all sorts of scary devices. Roger was supposed to be the ghost in the attic. He had practiced making hoots and howls and other eerie noises, and even went to the trouble of having a local seamstress make a spooky costume.

Underneath his outfit he would wear a leather harness with a rope and pulley. The pulley would hook onto a cable that stretched from one end of the attic to the other. When the timid little "ghouls" materialized in the attic, Roger would jump from his platform and "fly" through the air, shrieking with cries of the dead (he got into it as he rehearsed).

The night of the fund raiser came and Roger had been all set to play his part.

Only no one came upstairs.

He waited and waited, hearing sounds of conversation and laughter from the lower floors, but no costumed kids had found their way into his domain.

He decided to stay put. If he went downstairs now, he would give himself away.

About an hour into his stint, a young woman came walking across the attic floor. She was very attractive and well composed and introduced herself as a ghost. "OK," Roger grinned. "I'm one, too."

He went into detail about how he had rigged the cable and the vest. He told her about having the costume made specially for that evening and how he was a bit annoyed that no one had showed up after all the pains he'd taken.

The young woman was very pleasant. She listened attentively and laughed obligingly when his remarks were meant to amuse. Roger was glad he didn't have to sit out the evening alone. She in turn told how she had grown up in that old house, married her childhood sweetheart, and died from a broken heart. She told her story so well that he thought it was a real account drawn from someone else's history.

By the end of the evening, Roger was glad that someone downstairs had messed up. Laughing and chatting with this beautiful woman was much more enjoyable than facing a herd of screaming kids.

As noise from the lower floors began to die down, Roger decided to check and see what had gone wrong. "I'll just be a minute," he told his companion.

When he asked the chief organizer, the guy was obviously embarrassed. "Oh, I'm so sorry," he said. "I thought I had it covered. I guess no one told you we decided to scratch the ghost-on-a-pulley bit. At the last minute we realized some kid coulda gotten really scared. That's all we need is for some kid to break his neck bolting down the stairs in the dark."

"Well, you might at least have told the other 'ghost' you sent upstairs to let me know things were off. If it hadn't been for her, it would have been a very boring evening." Roger colored his voice with a little petulance that he didn't feel. He had, after all, enjoyed the evening.

"What other ghost?" the director said. "You were the only one assigned to the attic."

"Get off. Who are you trying to jive?" Roger turned back toward the stairs when his steps were arrested. Over the mantel hung a picture of a woman in Roaring Twenties garb. She was a dead ringer for the woman with whom he had spent the evening.

He headed for the attic. She was gone.

As he made his way back downstairs, the owner of the old house ambled through the front doorway. "Sir," Roger called, "who's the woman in the picture over the dining room mantle? The one with the green dress."

"That's my grandmother," the old man said. "She was born in this house, raised in this house, had her babies in this house, and died in this house. That was 1929. She was only 28 years old."

Roger was troubled. He didn't know if he had seen something or if he had known the story all along and his mind had just put things together.

What he did know was that he wasn't going to ask anybody, he wasn't going to tell anybody . . . and he wasn't going to try to find out any more.

*　　*　　*

"It was the British, I'm telling you," Roger poked a finger at Sam with a note of authority.

Tessie's ears perked up. She, too, felt that the British were responsible for all the problems in the Middle East, but she never had heard one of the goyim say it.

Roger continued to pontificate. "Decades ago the big petroleum companies and the British government used their power in the region, then left the place in a shambles after World War II. Now you've got western powers lining up to back one repressive government over another repressive government. If you had a contest to decide who was more brutal, the Iraqis or the Saudis, the race would be so close that not even a photo finish could settle it.

"Remember, these countries we've sided with have governments that won't let women drive cars. They cut off people's hands in public for stealing, and they don't tolerate any other religion."

Roger obviously was angry over the situation. His mention of a bloody public punishment steered Sam's mind back to what he was contemplating before Roger started yapping his opinions. *I wonder,* he thought, *if Saddam Hussein was one of my kind? Idi Amin certainly was. He practiced cannibalism on his victims.* Roger's droning voice provided a refuge into which Sam retreated with his most private dreams. He uttered a prayer to his lord Satan and began to fantasize about having sex with someone and, just before the climax, strangling them. Their death spasms would heighten his ecstasy. *I will disembowel them, wrap their entrails around my body, and dance to you, my Lord, as I drink their blood.*

"At least in Iraq there are 100,000 Christians who are free to choose their own religion. Even Prime Minister Azziz is a Christian, though not one I'd want anything to do with." Roger didn't care if a person was a Christian or not; he just thought if people had to be religious, at least they ought to be free to pick their poison.

By now he had built up a head of steam. "What are we doing there? Look at the risk we're taking—this could have turned into Armageddon."

Awakened from his reverie by the last statement, Sam shook his head in mock dismay as he silently gloated, *May you wallow in the blood of the slaughter, my Lord.*

Tessie Ginsberg only wondered.

The witch was attractive, 40-ish,
well-dressed and articulate . . .

---

3. THE WAY OF
THE WORLD TODAY

By the time Evelyn Thompson entered the teachers'
lounge to munch on her Weight Watchers dried fruit and
unwind a bit, Roger's oration had just about run its course.

"I don't know much about what you're referring to,"
Sam answered, "but I do know that the whole Middle East
is a mess that goes back thousands of years. You can't palm
it all off on the British. Sorry. I don't buy."

He pulled the paper up in front of his face, effectively
disconnecting himself from Roger and his opinions.

"Hi, guys!" Evelyn said. "What's up?" With a slight
nod in Sam's direction Evelyn looked straight at Roger and
rolled her eyes. Roger smirked. They all sensed unspoken
agreement—Sam might seem to have it all together, but he
was always so . . . detached, distant. Weird?

"Evelyn, what do you think about the problems in the
Middle East?" Roger knew she was always up for a lively
discussion.

Evelyn rose to the challenge. "I think it's an absolute
nightmare. They're positively ruining the planet. Imagine
the devastation caused by millions—no, tens of millions of

gallons of crude oil sprawling its black, oily goo over every beach and into every niche in the ecosystem for hundreds of miles.

"Then 950 oil fields burning in 'liberated' Kuwait! It will be years before they all are extinguished. Can you imagine the pollution that will cause?"

She was on a roll. "And we're just beginning to find out about the damage caused by the bombing! The military always scars the face of the earth and obliterates all life in its path."

In her mind, Evelyn added, *Crude, uncaring men clawing the delicate face of Geia, the Mother, Mother Earth.*

Evelyn has strong feelings about the recent conflicts in the Gulf region, not because she is interested in politics or religion. She's interested because she's deeply concerned about the earth.

For good reason. Evelyn was born in the Midwest on a farm. She worked alongside her parents as they nurtured and cultivated the land. Though they held deed to the place, they never really felt that they owned it. How can you divide and own something that had existed for millions and millions of years, eons before you were even born?

The earth knows how to give and how to take. It is a joy to cooperate in that process and watch the land yield its crops. It's a partnership, not ownership. That's how Evelyn always had thought of it.

When Evelyn went to the University of Washington at Seattle, she gave as much time and energy as she could to help worthy organizations fight for the environment, but she felt they were on the superficial side. Sometimes they seemed like no more than a gathering of do-gooders trying to be helpful to a cause they didn't understand. Sure, they cared about the environment, but they didn't see themselves as partners. They didn't love the earth for just itself, at least not the way she did.

This proved to be an ongoing source of frustration for her, even after she had moved down the coast to take a rather high-paying job as an executive assistant in a marketing firm. In fact, the marketing job seemed to exacerbate her frustration. She had trained to become a teacher because she always had wanted to be a teacher. She wanted young people to think and feel, to be responsive and responsible, to sense their own oneness with the planet.

Still, by the time graduation rolled around, she found herself distracted by what appeared to be more exciting opportunities, at least to a 21-year-old tired of school. Since that graduation, she felt more and more that she was cut off from her roots, alienated from her true concerns.

That is, until one day when she turned on a talk show produced by a local TV station.

They were interviewing a witch.

Or at least the host kept referring to her as a witch. The woman explained that, while she wouldn't necessarily describe herself as a witch, she wouldn't object if others called her that. The problem was that the word *witch* had grown some very unfortunate and misleading barnacles on its hull over the years, due mainly to popular stories that were no more than nonsense.

The well-spoken guest described the wicca or the coven and the principles to which they adhered. She spoke of preserving the earth and becoming one with nature. She emphatically stated that they had nothing to do with the casting of spells.

The witch was attractive, 40-ish, well-dressed and articulate in the way well-educated people are articulate—

very careful and precise, hoping to educate as well as inform.

"What about broom-riding?" the host had quipped to the delighted giggles of the studio audience. The woman just smiled and enjoyed the joke with them. Evelyn admired her confidence and composure.

Because she was lonely and looking for real soul-mates, and because the part about saving the earth had struck a responsive chord, Evelyn felt drawn to the talk-show guest. She wrote down the woman's name when it was repeated and called the TV station to find out how to get in touch with her.

With more than a little hesitation, she dialed the number given by the receptionist at the station. After all, she was calling a celebrity . . . or at least a person who was important enough to be interviewed on television.

Evelyn recognized the voice that answered the phone as that of the woman on the TV. She was just as warm and friendly as when she was being interviewed on the talk show. Evelyn was surprised, though later she laughed at herself for having been so timid. She felt such a kinship with this woman that she rattled on and on about how she admired her insight, her values and her courage to get on TV to speak about them.

"Thank you, Evelyn. You're so kind to take time to call and tell me," the voice replied. Her genuine appreciation made Evelyn self-conscious. She realized that she had been dominating the conversation. Her mother used to warn her about that.

But the woman hadn't seemed to mind. In fact, she had introduced herself with, "Please call me Amber." Here was this important person from television, not putting her off with a "let's do lunch sometime." Instead, Amber was taking time to talk to her in the midst of what must have been a busy schedule.

To Evelyn's utter amazement, Amber began trying to arrange a convenient time for the two of them to meet.

"Tell you what," Amber said. "Are you busy right now? Why don't I just come over? What's that address?"

Evelyn not only felt excitement, but she could also actually see her excitement in the slight tremble of her hand as she reached to open the door. Amber shook Evelyn's timid hand in greeting, and held it for an extra moment as she looked into her eyes and said, in all seriousness, "Your name isn't Evelyn any more. From now on it will be 'Emerald.' "

From that moment, Evelyn knew that she was no longer alone in her love for the earth. She had found someone who understood. Amber spent lots of time with "Emmy" (her new nickname). They talked about their concerns, their hopes, and their dreams for the planet. Evelyn felt that she had learned more from Amber in a few short weeks than she had in a lifetime.

Amber helped her realize that the entire authority structure of modern society fosters injustice. "Much of the problem stems from the whole idea of a patriarchal system," Amber explained. "It's not that all men are bad. In fact," she added with a smile and a twinkle in her eye, "some men are *quite* nice. But the whole business of submissiveness is a very male thing. It is a system that gave too much power to individuals who naturally became corrupted by it. Quite simply, that power corrupted absolutely and it led to abuse."

Evelyn, "Emmy," was enthralled. None of her Ag or Ed profs had tied the whole problem in such a simple knot. "You're right, Amber," she added. "We weren't meant to have that kind of power over one another—or over the earth."

"As for religion," Amber continued, "the whole notion of a transcendent 'God' is the absolute pinnacle of male tyranny. Notice how people, even most women, refer to divinity as 'He'? And aren't we admonished by a virtually all-male clergy that because 'He' has absolute power, we are all to be subservient and obey 'His' every command?"

Emmy was mesmerized, especially as Amber explained what *should* be. "We should respect the god and goddess in one another as we unite with all of creation, the real divinity."

As Amber expressed herself over the following weeks, Evelyn grew more and more dissatisfied with her job. It was so terribly mundane. She basically was a go-fer anyway, and she wasn't interested in advancing. She even began to feel violated by the job, almost that sales somehow prostituted her.

Her love life was only OK, too. She had tried different men, and if the truth were told, she had tried a couple of women, too. But nothing seemed to take. It just wasn't that hot.

But Evelyn liked people. She liked Amber from the start, and she melded into the wicca as if she had known the twelve other women all her life. She liked getting together regularly to sing songs of nature addressed to Mother Earth and Brother Tree and Sister Stream. She liked celebrating their oneness with creation and their love for the earth.

So when Evelyn lost her job at the marketing company she had mixed feelings. Actually, she was glad to be out of that work environment where people were viewed as objects with money, but she didn't like feeling so uncertain about her future. And she didn't like to think that she might have to move to a job in another city.

When Amber suggested that Emmy find a job as a schoolteacher, all the lights seemed to go on. It all fit together. "After all, that's what you're trained for," she said. "And think of the opportunity you'd have to help mold young people's attitudes about our planet."

That did it. Evelyn put together a resumé and began visiting the local school boards. On her second interview, she met Mr. McDonald. He was the personnel director for the Merit School District, and he hired her on the spot. Evelyn's few short years in business were a plus in McDonald's thinking.

With her new career, Evelyn could stay in town and become more involved in important causes. Her commitment to the wicca deepened. She felt that at last her life was taking on real meaning. It was becoming whole.

That's why Evelyn feels so strongly about the Middle East thing; to her it is the rape of the earth by geopolitical leaders and their minions.

"It's despicable," she announced to Roger and the others, "and I fully intend to fight it by participating in every public demonstration, ecology rally, and peace protest I can find."

Evelyn was not angry, not at her colleagues anyway. But she would take every opportunity to make her views known in no uncertain terms. She leaned over to Tessie and said, "Mrs. Ginsberg, what do you think? Or have these clods even bothered to ask?"

Tessie was not sure she wanted to answer. To her, more than anything else, the Middle East means Israel. She believes her people have a God-given right to a homeland exactly where they are. It's in the Bible. The Jewish Bible.

Despite her sweet nature it irked her when the goyim (Gentiles) called it the "Old Testament." Did they think the Hebrew Scriptures were obsolete?

She's not exactly sure where in the Bible it says that about the Jews and Israel, but the rabbis know, and that's good enough.

Tessie is a lifelong member of Hadassah and is proud that during all the years of her marriage, she and her David were always able, thank God, to afford an annual $1000 donation to help establish and maintain a Jewish homeland.

Still, she wasn't so sure she wanted to answer Evelyn's question. These were her colleagues, but they were also goyim, and she remembered well what her father had taught her. "You have to get along with them. You know they don't like you, but you smile pleasantly . . . " just like her father always had done in the little dry goods store he ran when she was a child.

There, among the goyim, she had learned to keep her thoughts to herself.

Tessie's mother and father operated their small store in a changing neighborhood. They knew which customers were Jewish and which were not, but they were pleasant to everyone who set foot in their store and they treated each person with honesty and fairness.

At the same time, Tess had seen the rude, cold nature of many of the goyim. She had seen them laugh when someone was hurt. She saw some of them abandon their families when times got bad. On more than one occasion she heard goyim, so-called Christians, ask her father for a "Jewish bargain." She had overheard them bragging and laughing with one another about how they had "Jewed the old Hebe down."

Then there was the time Tessie's father had to fire a lazy clerk whom he caught stealing from the store. As he stomped out the door the man had turned and yelled, "You BLEEP, BLEEP dirty Jew!"

Her father had turned to Tessie, and quietly said, "You see?"

And Tessie did see. That was the way life was for Jews among Gentiles, so she wasn't sure she wanted to answer Evelyn's question. The reawakened emotion of past hurts seemed to explode of its own accord, though, and she found herself saying, "The British? Let them go to the devil!"

Sam looked up from his paper and nodded with a smile.

"What do they expect from Israel?" Tessie continued. "To bomb Israel, to send their spook missiles, or . . . or . . . whatever they call them, that they should come down and blow up more Jewish children? And we should sit still for this after everything else . . . ?"

*"We ain't lookin' for the undertaker.
We're lookin' for the Uppertaker."*

---

4. THE WAY
OF THE WORLD
TOMORROW

About the time Tessie Ginsberg realized she was saying more than she intended to, Lovelle Williams sailed into the room wearing her perpetual smile. "What in the world are you people talking about that you've got sweet little Tessie here so fired up?"

"It's the Middle East, and the British, and the ecology, and the suffering Jews and the whole screwed-up world," Sam said from behind his newspaper.

"Uh-huh," Lovelle nodded her head with a serious but not frowning face. "I can see that. And wouldn't you know that one more time, I'm missing out on a good discussion."

And does Lovelle Williams ever love a good discussion! "It's food for the mind," she says to her class when they're a bit too self-conscious to speak up. She is completely dedicated to the teenagers in her classes. She wants for them, as well as her two daughters, the best the world has to offer and she sees a well-disciplined mind as a key that helps unlock the world's treasures.

The reason she feels so strongly about her students and about expressing herself clearly and often is that, for too many years, she missed out on life's treasures. At 45, with a little more tummy than she needs or wants, she has had more than her share of hard knocks.

To this day she doesn't know who her father was. Her mother cleaned other people's houses and worked the night shift in a biscuit factory to keep a roof over their heads.

In spite of the odds, Lovelle managed to start high school. But a fine, sweet-talkin' man sweet-talked her right into bed. By her 16th birthday she had one child in diapers and another on the way; by her 17th she was abandoned by her "husband"; and by the time her 18th birthday rolled around Lovelle was turning tricks to support her baby daughters and herself.

She did it for a while, but she knew it was wrong and she just could not continue to live that kind of life. Her mother had raised her better. So Lovelle left the streets and began working as a cleaning lady to provide for LaKesha and Olanda.

It was in that period in her life that everything changed. She felt very strongly that she had to "get right with God," so she and the girls started attending the church of her childhood, Mt. Gethsemane Missionary Baptist Church.

She also started reading. That had been a problem for her when she was in high school. But she determined that, if she was ever going to make anything of herself, she had to learn to read and to read well.

First it was the Bible. As she read it she found herself reflecting time and again: *Well Lord, I think I get the message.* And she did. It often seemed that God was sending thoughts her way.

She also read what other people—educated people—had to say about life, what's good and bad, what it all means. It began when she got in the habit of reading children's-level biographies of famous people to the girls. Soon her curiosity grew and so did her reading level. She began reading adult biographies. Then she graduated to what the famous people themselves had to say, especially the philosophers.

She loved the philosophers. They opened whole new worlds of thought and they gave her whole new ways of thinking about the world.

But always, she came back to the simple words of the Bible and the simple sermons delivered every Sunday by the barely literate pastor of Mt. Gethsemane Church. To her, they were whole. They made complete sense. While she loved the ideas she found in her famous authors, she always felt that they only gave half a picture—the human half. Only in the Bible had she found "the other half."

Lovelle likes to refer to her teen years as her "B.C. days," her days "Before Christ." She is unashamedly a Christian, a deaconess in her church (where they call her Sister Williams). She is always praising the Lord for "all His blessings and for allowing me to raise two good girls."

The funny thing is, Lovelle has every reason to feel just the opposite. Even when she was rediscovering God, the hard knocks kept coming. Unfortunately, almost all of them came from white people.

The truth is, Lovelle feels the same about white people as Tessie feels about non-Jews. As far as Lovelle is concerned, her people "never got anything good from white folks, but God love 'em anyhow, because the sweet Lord Jesus said, 'Bless those who revile you and spitefully use you.' " (She quotes Scripture about as well as Tevya in

Fiddler on the Roof, but people get the general idea and no one seems to know or care.)

Lovelle remembers being spitefully used. First it was her no-good husband. Then her johns. Then it was the white ladies she worked for. Some of them would kindly inform her that the only way to wash a floor was to "get down on your knees and use a scrub brush."

There was no shame for her in scrubbing another woman's dirty floors on her hands and knees. It was honest work and she was supporting her girls. Her own mother had done that very thing.

No, there was no shame in any of it until she ran up against the cruelty of one particular white woman. The rent was due and she only needed to do one more floor to earn the last $15. She had gotten every possible welfare grant and government aid, but her part still was a burden for her.

So she was happy to have the extra work.

It was a job for Eunice Edwards, the woman who first told Lovelle that the only way to wash a floor was to do it on your knees. So, when Lovelle entered the Edwards's kitchen, she headed for the bucket and the scrub brush in the cleaning closet, then got down to business—on her knees.

She was just beginning to make good headway when the Edwards woman moved quietly into the room. She paused motionless behind Lovelle, watching like an eagle ready to plummet to earth for its innocent prey. "Mrs. Williams, you've been working a full fifteen minutes and you only have half this floor done? I don't need any lazy niggers around my house. If you don't work faster, you don't have a job."

Lovelle pursed her lips and tried to work faster, but she didn't know how to do a poor job, so she just scrubbed harder. Ten minutes later, Mrs. Edwards came back. In a slow, deliberate voice she said, "Well I'm not sure we can keep you. I will *never* understand what is wrong with people of your race."

At that precise moment, all the pain and all the stress and all the frustration Lovelle had ever endured seemed to come crashing down. She took that pail of dirty water and threw it on Eunice Edwards, drenching her with all of the anger that all of the black people through all the years of abuse had ever felt at the injustice of life.

In the days that followed her outburst, Lovelle was very ashamed. She viewed that act of hatred as being just as evil as the prostitution of her teen years. As far as she was concerned, selling your body to a man for his gratification was no worse than selling your soul to anger for your own gratification.

She knew that from the Bible, and she also knew that God would forgive her if she asked.

As distressing as the incident with Mrs. Edwards was, it marked a turning point for Lovelle. In spite of the fact that she went back to Eunice Edwards, apologized, and asked for her forgiveness, word got out and she lost all but one of her regulars. Her income dried up and so did her courage.

Then one of the deacons in her church heard about an experimental welfare program designed to help young single mothers go to college. Lovelle went right out and enrolled. It was her dream—not merely to read what educated people had to say, but to *be* an educated person.

Seven long years and many sleepless nights later, she was a teacher. Her two girls had watched their mama take charge of her own life and now they had choices that she'd never had. Yes, by the Lord's grace she made it, and she's proud of it. She loves to tell people that she thanks and praises God every day, first for her salvation at 19 years of age when she was headed for a certain hell, and then for her church who upheld her and supported her, and for the Lord Jesus Christ who gave her this job in this school, and the fruit of His Spirit which will keep her from ever throwing a pail of washwater on anyone, anywhere, ever again.

*   *   *

"Let me tell you what I think," Lovelle said to the other teachers in the lounge. "All that's happening centers around Israel because we're living in the end times. These things in the Middle East are just a warm-up to Armageddon. But we ain't lookin' for the undertaker. We're lookin' for the Uppertaker—Jesus is coming soon." Lovelle is an intelligent woman and speaks perfect English in her classroom. But when she starts to talk about her Lord, she's more concerned with emphasis than with grammar.

Now when Lovelle Williams was hired at Merit High School, she made it a point to visit every teacher in the building. She wanted to get to know them all by name and to tell them what the Lord Jesus meant to her.

So everyone in that teachers' lounge knew exactly where she was coming from.

"The Lord Jesus is comin' with a shout and He's gonna blow his trumpet. Umm, umm!" Lovelle is powerfully impressed by first impressions, a holdover from her B.C. days when she couldn't read very well. She remembers things the way she hears them the first time. The problem is, she listens to a barely literate preacher who knows just enough of the Scripture to misquote it, and she carries on the misquotes.

" . . . and when He comes back, He's gonna deal with a man just like Saddam Hussein whose name is Antichrist and whose number is 666!"

Tessie wondered why Lovelle didn't finish the number. Maybe it was just the area code. She'd ask her later.

"You know what it means—all this attack on Israel and the nations gathering against I-raq," she pronounced it "eye-rak," another first impression. "It's a sign of the times. Didn't ya ever read about what the book of Revelations said about that Babylon? You know I-raq is ancient Babylon.

"Let me take a minute and tell you and you see if this doesn't come true. The next thing, all those nations that are gathered against I-raq are gonna come against Israel." She was getting excited now.

"Just you mark my words; this is gonna come to pass because it is prophesied that in the last days all the nations are gonna come agai . . . " she shifted her thought in mid-sentence, "and let me tell you why they're gonna come against Israel. They're gonna come against Israel because our President of these United States, Mr. George Bush— God bless 'im—has agreed and said that there's gonna be a peace talk.

"The United States of America and the Union of Socialist Soviet Republics," she loves to pronounce the entire names of the countries, even if she isn't quite correct, because she's a history teacher, "are gonna agree and call for a peace conference.

"Do you know what they're gonna do at that peace conference? Those Ay-rabs that have been pestering Isra .
. . " she shifted thoughts again, "Do you want to know about those Ay-rabs? It was those Ay-rabs, those Muslims, who went into black Africa and took those tribal people and sold them to the shipmasters. Those same Ay-rabs have the same heart against the Jews and you know the Jews are God's chosen people."

By this time, Tessie Ginsberg was enthralled. She never had heard one of the goyim, let alone one of the schvartzes, talk about the Jews being God's chosen people. But it was also how Lovelle Williams was saying it. Tessie was deeply impressed by the conviction and power and intelligence behind the rough dialect into which Lovelle had slipped. *There's much more to this woman than meets the eye,* she thought.

Evelyn was listening carefully, too, although not for the same reason. She had heard the preachers of her childhood talk about Jesus in their insipid sermons. But she had never heard Jesus mentioned in this frame of reference. Part of her was utterly repulsed by the idea of a God who could somehow be involved in the horrid muddle brought about by brutal male political leaders. She was repulsed by the idea of a God separate from the creation. She recalled what Amber had taught her about hierarchy as a tool of the oppressors against the oppressed. But another part of her was fascinated by the idea that somehow God *might* be able to control these dangerous events and that Jesus would return to rescue the planet.

Roger, by now parked on the couch next to Sam, was not even trying to hide a yawn. What started as an interesting discussion was rapidly deteriorating into a lecture on religion. As for God, Roger simply is not interested. He figures that in the rather unlikely event that there is a God who created the earth, He must be a royal screwup. He's sure not done His job very well. And Roger hates God-talk and sin-talk—too many people use it to excuse themselves from their responsibilities to society.

Sam, on the other hand, was absolutely spellbound. He believes in the end times. He believes in principalities and powers and spirits at work in the events of human history. He believes that there will be a judgment of fire on all the damned, including himself, and he relishes the thought. The flames, the pain, the sweet anguish. "My Lord Satan," he muttered to himself.

"I don't have to tell you I'm not Jewish," Lovelle continued with a swagger but without a trace of humor in her voice. "I believe that in the bottom of my heart—the Jews are God's chosen people.

"Anyhow, in that day, when all nations come against Jerusalem just like it's prophesied in the book of Zechariah in the Old Testament of the Holy Bible," Roger got up and headed for the door with a bored and detached goodbye wave, "God Himself is gonna go forth and He is gonna fight for the Jewish people.

"I'll tell you something else, too. This whole earth is moaning and groaning under the sinfulness of people. And when the Lord Jesus comes back, He's going to make a new heaven and a new earth and He'll see to it that no one ever messes with His creatures or His creation again. No more polluting, no more exploitation. 'Every knee shall bow and every tongue confess that Jesus Christ is Lord.' "

Evelyn was gripped. She always had viewed religion as the tool of a sexist society. Is it possible that there really is a God other than Mother Earth who cares about it and the horrid injustice that is so rampant? Is it possible that He . . . no, She . . . no . . . well, is it possible that being could somehow invade history?

"Let me tell you one more thing. We are all educated people, but we are not educated enough until we read the Word of God . . . "

Only one source claims to be
the self-revelation of God.

---

5. SEARCHING FOR LIGHT IN DARK SAYINGS

Do you know a Sam Trevanti? Depending on what part of the country you live in or what line of work you're in, you may have met him several times and never recognized him. Or he may be no more real to you than a fairy tale.

But what about Tessie Ginsberg? She's the grandmotherly lady just down the street, isn't she?

And Roger? He's everywhere.

The fact is, the people you just met—Lovelle, Evelyn, Roger and the rest—are us! They may have different colored skin or a different background, or a very different secret life, but they are still us—people trying to make sense of sometimes senseless global events, like the invasion of Kuwait or the decades-long tension in the Middle East.

You read the headlines, watch the CNN reports, listen to the experts, and still . . .

... and still get the sense that behind it all there may be something or somebody else at work. You feel it, intuitively, but you can't put your finger on it. Like the people profiled in the first four chapters, you're looking for spiritual reality and certainty in an unreal, uncertain world.

JUST BEHIND THE VEIL

The alarm jars you into semi-consciousness. You stumble into the bathroom, then head for the kitchen.

You fix your morning brew, grab your favorite mug and maybe spread a little butter and jam on an English muffin. You brave the early morning chill just long enough to snatch the newspaper. Returning to the kitchen, you plop down, ready to begin your morning ritual.

First, the headlines—a quick scan. Nothing new. Then the obits. No one you know. Next the comics. They thought that was funny? And just to amuse yourself, you take a quick look at the daily horoscope.

You don't really believe in horoscopes, but they're kind of like the comics—caricatures of life—except that very often they really do seem to describe you. It doesn't happen every time and you figure it's probably just coincidence when it does.

Maybe not, though.

Anyway, it's no big deal. You've been around long enough to know that there are certain things beyond understanding.

Like the guy who had planned a trip to Chicago months ago. He even bought his ticket two months in advance. Then at the last minute he had the strangest feeling (he wouldn't call it a premonition) that he absolutely should not go.

A few of his colleagues had smirked to think that such an otherwise sensible guy would change his plans on a whim.

No one smirked when they heard that half the people aboard that flight had been killed in a plane crash. Yes, you've seen enough to know there are some things that just can't be explained, at least not by anything we know of.

Tessie, Lovelle, Sam, Evelyn—they all recognize it. And you have sensed it, too. It's an intuition, an awareness that just beyond the veneer of space and time lies another reality. You sense that in light of that reality, all the inexplicable fragments of human life fit together into a bigger picture than we presently can perceive or believe.

You know that the real news is not what someone else decides we'll read in the *Wall Street Journal* or the *Los Angeles Times*. You know that the real meaning of what goes on is not exposed in the features stories of *20/20* or *60 Minutes*.

It's true. There's a whole spiritual realm of forces and antiforces in which the issues of life are resolved; where a person is affected for inner peace, for ultimate reality and for eternal destiny.

The ancients sensed it—but their half-knowledge often was shrouded in superstition.

What of us today? Realizing that much of what passed for "ancient powers" was blatant manipulation, we consider ourselves intellectually sophisticated and far beyond the "bogeyman" mentality.

For centuries we moderns have derided and rejected anything that cannot be tested empirically and proved. Yet in recent times those thoughts, events and hints of "something more" have surfaced again.

SOULS AWAKENING

You have to awaken to that other world just as you awaken to this world every morning. You have been asleep, unconscious to your environment and to all that has been occurring in the night hours.

As you begin to stir, you hear sounds. You become aware of smells, you sense whether it's daylight or still dark. When you rise, your vision isn't quite clear. Things are blurry. You move around in a fog, until in the bathroom you bend over the sink and clean your eyes.

Then you begin to see what's really there.

From the Shamans of the ancients to the crystal carriers of the New Age, from the mystics of the Orient to the black Muslims on the streets of New York, it's surprisingly the same. These are souls who have been aroused to discover that there is something beyond the events of this life.

Yet many souls who begin to awaken to that unseen world end up wandering in the blur and the fog all their lives. They are constantly looking for the "spiritual water" that will wash the sleep of the physical world from their inner eyes so they can see.

THE VIEW FROM A HIGHER PLANE

One of the characteristics these people share is an enhanced perception of history. They are on a higher plane of awareness from which they can look down on the landscape of time and see a pattern from the beginning to the end.

This amplified consciousness also gives such people a different perception of the future. While they have yet to read the last chapter, they often sense where "the story" is headed. The desire for this heightened consciousness motivates many other people to search for it in a number of places and in various ways.

For example, one local Jewish Community Center's Institute for Jewish Living and Learning recently ran an ad for a course to be taught at the Center:

A BASIC TRAINING IN JEWISH SPIRITUALITY: DIVINITY IN OURSELVES

Whatever your life path has been until now, this series will meet you where you stand and help bring you home to yourself. Come and be prepared to join the joyous community for Jewish renewal.

What we know about the God within the self the group teaches us on the inside. How to access this "intuition" can be learned. The schools of Jewish Mysticism taught these processes. We will practice some of them and make them portable for our use.

The processes referred to in the ad are part of a tradition called Kabbalah. A brochure from the Research Centre of Kabbalah describes the tradition this way:

Kabbalah has been the hidden knowledge of Judaism. It defines the cosmic laws of the universe and delineates how to apply these principles practically into daily life. Through applying this knowledge to our lives, not only can we achieve personal fulfillment, we can also achieve global harmony.

Kabbalah invites each individual to experience directly the vast inner spiritual power available to everyone. With the knowledge of these inner resources and the application of fundamental Kabbalistic principles, we can actually achieve mastery over our destiny and fulfillment in our lives.

The media reports this general reawakening to spiritual things as though it were new. The only thing new about it is that, while in the past individuals garnered personal profit from people's interest in the spiritual, now we have entire industries growing up around it.

IT'S RIGHT WHERE PEOPLE LIVE

But today, like every other day in human history, ordinary people like you and me are looking for answers. Which one of us wouldn't want to clear the sleep from our eyes and make more sense of this life?

Rosalee (not a fictitious character) is a good example. One day I stopped by the deli that Rosalee and her late husband established twenty-four years ago. Rosalee is probably 70 years old. She'd be the first to describe herself as "no spring chicken," but she still works hard.

She's always there at the deli to greet people with a cheerful smile, especially on the weekends when they have six people behind the counter slicing cappicola and provolone, packaging the fresh pasta and ladling the mouth-watering sauces into take-away containers.

Rosalee treats everyone who walks through the door like an old friend.

She's the only one behind the counter wearing a name badge, so when it's my turn I call her by name. "So, Rosalee, what's good today?"

"The frittata. Here, take a bite. This is the zucchini. It's my favorite." She pauses to watch me chew and swallow, then, "Here, try the asparagus."

"How much?"

"It goes by the piece, $4.95 a pound." Her knife is poised to slice.

"I think I like the first one better. It's spicier. Give me about a pound."

"Yeah, I like that one too." With her other hand Rosalee deftly reaches for the zucchini frittata in the display case.

"Rosalee, you're a common-sense person. Let me ask you a question. Fortune tellers . . . what do you think?"

A shadowed expression crosses Rosalee's face and her smile goes somewhere else for a moment. She leans toward me and says in a quiet voice, "I believe in fortune tellers. One time, when I was in my early 30s, I went to one. I wore gloves so she couldn't see that I wasn't married. She didn't know me and she told me that in six months I would be married."

Rosalee's voice brightens and the smile returns. "Well, it was seven months, not six. I was married in June, not May, but it's all the same. Yes, I believe in fortune tellers."

She returns to my frittata.

"What about curses?" I ask.

This time Rosalee's whole face grows dark as she raises her head and slowly nods an affirmative, "Curses. Yes."

"Was it by a priest or from a dark woman?"

She mutters something I can't quite hear under her breath, concluding with a shudder and a barely audible " . . . and the person died!" She was oblivious to my second question.

So I ask again. "A priest or a dark woman?"

"A woman . . . in my childhood." She shakes her head firmly. "No. I won't talk about it."

TOOLS OF SOCIETY OR TOOLS FOR MANIPULATION?

Ordinary people don't trust the tools of a secular society. They've listened to psychologists on television who said that children were undergoing tremendous personal trauma because of the war in the Persian Gulf. They remember that before the war those same psychologists were saying that those same children were undergoing tremendous personal trauma because of an earthquake, or a tornado.

And they remember when they were children during World War II, or the Cuban missile crisis, or the Vietnam War. They remember that they were scared, maybe even terrified, but they were not undergoing tremendous personal trauma.

What they trust is what their mothers told them, what their neighbors confirmed, and what they could see with their own eyes. What they don't trust are the professorial types who make pronouncements about the nature of reality — which just happens to change with the trends of time.

They know there are spirits. They know there's something to astrology. They know there is "karma," "good luck and bad luck," and much more.

So, as unscientific as it might seem, many people are reaching out into realms they regard as being spiritual. Do crystals bring inner harmony? Does chanting a mantra really make you feel at one with all the earth? Do the rhythmic breathing of yoga or the tantric exercises of Buddhism really make you more adept at sexual performance? Do these things really help?

"Yes! Yes! Yes!" whisper a multitude of people.

While modern science is appreciated and definitely not rejected, empirical knowledge simply is not enough. That's why a person can have a Ph.D. in physics yet go to meetings to discuss flying saucers.

That's why a physician who is considering buying into a real estate syndicate puts his hand on the salesman's forearm and asks, "What's your sign?" Then he sheepishly explains that he doesn't believe in such things but his wife does.

That's why we know intuitively that the spiritual world is far greater than that which can be comprehended with our five senses.

SCIENCE PROVES!

We do appreciate science. It has done many wonderful things for us. But while it can brew our coffee faster, help us grow more crops on less land, and ameliorate the effects of some diseases, it cannot provide the answer for anything beyond its own natural home, the realm of the empirical.

When I was a boy we heard over and over again, "Science proves . . . " This was usually followed by the speaker's offer of a conclusion which then became an assumption from which moral values were drawn.

An example. One of the bromides that shaped the educational system in days past was: "Science proves that children learn best when they are allowed to associate freely with one another in a classroom rather than sit uncomfortably in one place where they must learn things by rote memory and recite back to the teacher." Upon this premise was built a whole system of education called Progressive Education.

When, as a child, I went to cheder (private Hebrew school), I learned axiomatic truths by rote, definitely an outmoded method by the standards of the Progressive

Education advocates. When I went to Denver public schools, I was immersed in a system of Progressive Education where, until the third grade, we did what we wanted to do. In the fourth and fifth grades we were required to do a few things, but never any homework.

All the way through junior high, I never had a homework assignment, because it was believed that children would learn better through free association and exposure to knowledge.

As a result of Progressive Education, I never learned the multiplication tables above 6; however, I still know those axiomatic truths I learned in cheder as a very young child. The many concepts and words that I didn't fully understand at the time now are filled with meaning. They were like empty vehicles parked inside my mind, waiting to be loaded with the freight of meaning I would gain through the experiences of my life.

OUR FILTERING SYSTEMS

The end result of decades of the "Science as Savior" view is that now, when something is offered authoritatively, one does not necessarily accept it. We have developed a filtering system, a series of grids made up of our own values, which serves to screen all that is presented to us. When we read something in the newspapers or hear it on a TV report, we believe only those things that make it through our filtering system. Unfortunately, this same filtering system can give rise to a serious handicap, because there are truths that are simply too big to go through our filters. Do miracles happen? If so, how would one know?

When we come across questions like that, the tendency is to force them through the grids we use to understand ordinary events. Even when we experience a miracle firsthand, our filtering system works retroactively, affecting our memory of the event if it cannot block out the event itself. What at first seems to be an invasion of the natural by the supernatural, over time, becomes more an allegation of our memory than an act of reality.

It's a problem we all deal with, even those of us who have long since recognized the existence of the unseen.

The dilemma is only sharpened as we look to experiences to provide us with a better perspective. Experiences are ephemeral. They provide no sure basis for the restructuring of the grids in our filtering system. What happens and is real today becomes a memory or a question mark in light of what is real tomorrow.

While I am aware that this is one way to construct a filtering system, it seems to me to be about as fruitful as a desert sheik's attempt to build a desalination plant on the rolling surface of the ocean. It may be close to the water, but . . .

Peter, the Galilean peasant who left his fishing nets to follow Jesus, another "Galilean peasant," had to deal with this very problem of experience as a reliable foundation for life. The story is recorded in the Gospel of Mark in the New Testament:

> After six days Jesus took Peter, James and John with him and led them up a high mountain, where they were all alone. There he was transfigured before them. His clothes became dazzling white, whiter than anyone in the world could bleach them. And there appeared before them Elijah and Moses, who were talking with Jesus.
>
> Peter said to Jesus, "Rabbi, it is good for us to be here. Let us put up three shelters—one for you, one for Moses and one for Elijah." (He did not know what to say, they were so frightened.)
>
> Then a cloud appeared and enveloped them, and a voice came from the cloud: "This is my Son, whom I love. Listen to him!"

Suddenly, when they looked around, they no longer saw anyone with them except Jesus (Mark 9:2-8).

If ever anyone had an occasion and a reason for faith arising out of personal experience, Peter did. He observed many of the miracles that Jesus performed, but the most awe-inspiring was the one recorded above.

Peter saw the old and the new come together. He saw the glory of Jesus, the Shekinah glory of God radiating from Him. Peter was gripped with fear, but was so drawn to the majestic display that he stammered, "Let's stay here."

It was a watershed event in his life.

Yet the reality of that momentous event, the memory of that miracle in Peter's personal experience, was not enough to keep him from denying this same Jesus in the moment of trial.

Decades after the event, when Peter was very near death, he wrote to believers who also were enduring their moments of trial. To them he mentioned this event in his life:

> I will endeavor that ye may be able after my decease to have these things always in remembrance. For we have not followed cunningly devised fables, when we made known unto you the power and coming of our Lord Jesus Christ, but were eyewitnesses of his majesty. For he received from God the Father honour and glory, when there came such a voice to him from the excellent glory, "This is my beloved Son, in whom I am well pleased." And this voice which came from heaven we heard, when we were with him in the holy mount.
>
> We have also a more sure word of prophecy; Whereunto ye do well that ye take heed, as unto a light that shineth in a dark place, until the day dawn, and the day star arise in your heart (2 Peter 1:15-19, KJV).

It is significant that Peter did not tell those people living under terrific strain to pray for the experience of a miracle similar to the one he had enjoyed. Just a miracle, only a vision. A little one, God. Please?

They did need something to disclose God to them, some sort of prophetic vision of a hidden God who really cares and really is in control.

But a miracle in and of itself just wouldn't cut it.

Experiences make sorry foundations for the building of one's life. Peter had learned that the hard way.

Instead of urging them to seek glimpses of the supernatural through experiences such as his, Peter pointed his readers to "a more sure word of prophecy."

That "more sure word" not only would reveal God to them in their time of need, but also would be the kind of stable, trustworthy, unchanging revelation, a sure foundation, upon which they could safely construct their day-to-day lives.

It's no different today. We all are in search of this spiritual reality. We sometimes look for it in "dark" or obscure sayings, because in the shadows of mysteries we perceive a glimmer of light. Or we seek a miracle and often find it, hoping it will once and for all clear the sleep out of our waking eyes. Or we look to a harmonic convergence in which we hope to experience the coming together of all the disparate forces at work inside ourselves.

But the person genuinely seeking spiritual reality — the sleep being washed from the eyes — must, if he (or she) is intellectually honest, consider the only source that claims to be the self-revelation of God. It alone claims to be the "more sure word of prophecy." It alone claims to be able to "make you wise unto salvation."

The Word of God. Can it be trusted? Let's see.

Of 737 predicted events, more than
two-thirds have been fulfilled.

---

6. THE MORE SURE WORD OF PROPHECY

Could Lovelle Williams possibly know about the future—just from reading her Bible?

One thing is certain. Of all the people in the Merit High School teachers' lounge, Lovelle Williams is the only one whose quest for spiritual reality has turned up any clear vision of that future.

And she is not alone. For centuries, the educated and uneducated alike have discovered who God is, what He has done, what He will do, and what He expects of us—all in the pages of this ancient revelation. Scientific and archaeological discoveries have only served to confirm what seekers like Lovelle already know: The Bible is reliable.

In the Jewish Scripture (Christians call this the Old Testament), we have the record of God revealing Himself in the past. Not only did God make certain that these acts were recorded, but He also instructed the Jewish people to memorialize His acts of redemption from generation to generation.

That is why we continually have looked back on significant events and have celebrated them with feasts and songs and holy days. The accounts of the exodus of the Hebrew slaves from Egypt, the crossing of the Red Sea, the giving of the Law to Moses—all were (and are) habitually repeated to remind people of God's revelation of Himself through His mighty acts on behalf of His people.

What of God's revelation for us, in the here and now? Time after time in the Scripture, God reveals Himself as "our refuge and strength, a very present help in trouble" (Psalm 46:1, KJV), or "I am the LORD your God." In fact, one needn't go any further than "The LORD is my shepherd; I shall not want" (Psalm 23:1) to catch a glimpse of how God peels away all but the present moment to divulge Himself today.

Those who have sensed that an encounter with the Almighty must be on His terms, not ours, have found the Bible to be an incredibly dynamic book which reveals everything we need to know about God and us.

What about the future? Has He revealed himself there? Absolutely! Scripture is filled with word of what He will do in human history yet to be written.

If you are concerned about what will happen in the days to come, there are two crucial questions you'll want to ask now if you haven't already done so. The **first** is:

What has God revealed about the future?

The **second** and equally important question is:

Why hasn't He revealed more?

Let's deal with the second question here and save the first for the final section of this book.

WHY HASN'T GOD REVEALED MORE ABOUT THE FUTURE?

You could consider God the master psychologist. He created us and He knows us. He knows what we can handle and what we can't handle.

Here's an example. For argument's sake, let's say you believe in heaven. The Bible does have some things to say about heaven, but on the whole the references are abstract and somewhat vague.

Can you imagine what life would be like if we had a clear-cut idea of what heaven is like? Our lives, our duties, our relationships, and whatever we might be responsible for on this earth would become utterly unbearable in the light of that glory (heaven). We would be so intent on getting to that perfect place that we would neglect the world and the people around us here and now.

But because God only hinted at what lies ahead for those who love Him, we can live fully in this world with all its pain and joy. At the same time, we can still have hearts brimming with the hope of the life to come.

However, according to the Scripture, not everything in the future is that bright, especially for those who have not yet been reconciled to their Maker. If we were to know more of the time and place and details of the future this earth is hurtling toward, we might be paralyzed with terror or spin out into a chaotic frenzy.

God in His mercy does not disclose everything.

But by that same mercy, God sometimes provides a fleeting glance through the veil of time. When that happens, it sobers us to our present reality. It informs us as to the nature of the forces in our world. It heartens us to live for Him with enthusiasm and commitment.

These fleeting glimpses are sprinkled throughout the Scripture. One biblical scholar indexed these, arranged them in the chronological order of their fulfillment, and numbered them. He catalogued prophecies of 737 specific events contained in 8480 verses of the Bible. Each of the 737 events are prophesied in at least one place in the Bible, and many are honored with prophesies found in several places.

Of those 737 events, more than two-thirds have been fulfilled. They were future events at the time of their delivery, but have found consummation in the course of time.[1]

However, a significant number of these prophesied events remain to be fulfilled in our future.

THE BIBLE—A GLIMPSE THROUGH THE VEIL

What are those prophecies for the future? To discover that, you must dig deep into those pages and mine from the truth that's there.

Unfortunately, many people balk when it comes to doing such mining, not because they aren't interested but because they are intimidated. A way to overcome that intimidation is to learn a bit about the Bible and its prophecy.

The Bible is not a long list of precepts, or a thousand-page version of the Ten Commandments.

Most of it is narrative—stories describing how ordinary people lived their lives and how God was active among nations as well as with individuals. These narratives are as helpful as the laws and precepts found in Scripture. The laws and precepts are abstract, the stories are concrete. That is the nature of the Bible.

And because the Bible does tell us something about the future, we—like the people in those narratives—have the opportunity to align ourselves with God in each of our tomorrows.

Be very certain about this point. God means for people like Tessie Ginsberg and Sam Trevanti—and you—to realize that He has not left His world in the dark about His intentions. In biblical prophecy, God has spoken, like it or not, accept it or not.

If the Bible does allow glimpses through the veil, why has it become fashionable for many so-called theologians to disclaim any knowledge of the book of Daniel or Revelation or other prophecy in the Bible? "I can't figure it out" has become a sign of modesty, virtue and wisdom.

Well, ignorance is never a virtue.

God never would give us anything He didn't intend for us to understand. If people don't understand the book of Revelation, it is simply because, as with miracles, they have not allowed it through their filtering system. Many people simply will not take into their understanding certain disturbing facts that do not fit in with what they have already decided to believe.

JUST WHAT IS PROPHECY, ANYWAY?

If you have a genuine desire to explore what the Scripture says about the future, there are two important prerequisites. **First,** you need to change the "filter" in your system to allow something beyond your ordinary experience to come through; and **second,** you need to understand the nature of prophecy in the Scripture.

You might imagine that biblical prophecy is akin to a Jeanne Dixon-type prophecy, i.e., the prediction of coming events for the sake of having predicted them. Her predictions were as far from biblical prophecy as the east is from the west.

Had Jeanne Dixon been a prophet in biblical times, she wouldn't have made it past her first season. At the peak of her career her predictions came true only about 20 percent of the time. Dixon's prognostications made her a "profit," but not a "prophet."

A real prophet, one from the biblical periods, had to bat 1000 or pay for striking out with his life.

Then there's the Nostradamus-type of prophet, the kind who utters dark sayings filled with complicated ramifications. While not as superficial as the first type, such "prophets" still have a fundamental problem. In their sayings we perceive flashes of truth, but they are buried in a dark, amorphous mass of words whose sum total doesn't add up to much. It can be great fun to read Nostradamus, but you come out on the other side no better off than when you went in.

No, biblical prophecy is different—very different. First of all, the predictive element always is secondary. In moving the spirit of the prophet to speak or write to His people, God was not primarily interested in revealing the future. When He did reveal the future, it was to accomplish far more than the mere assuaging of people's natural curiosity.

Prophecy was never intended as a cosmic peep show.

PROPHECY ALWAYS WAS ABOUT THE PRESENT

The first thing you need to know about prophecy is that when God revealed Himself through the prophets, His primary purpose was to speak to His people about their present situation. He was and is interested in having relationships with people who want to know how they should live in the present.

God is not impressed with a bevy of religious people spouting a lot of future talk with little regard for what should be happening right now.

The message God had for the "present situation" of the ancients was either positive or negative. The negative message often was like a parent-child disciplinary interchange, a warning of some kind: Cease doing that or there will be severe consequences; detour and head in another direction and I will come to your aid.

That is why prophecies often were given to kings, who were presumably in a position to act responsibly and influence the nation. On occasion, the prophecy was given after the fact, to point out that wrong had been committed and that God was about to bring judgment.

For example, when King David had one of his faithful soldiers killed to cover up the fact that he had made the man's wife pregnant, the prophet Nathan visited him. He told the king a story of a rich man who confiscated a poor man's only sheep so he could entertain guests at no expense to himself. When David exploded in anger and vowed to right this grievous wrong, Nathan looked at him and said, "You are the man!"

That is biblical prophecy without a shred of the future in it.

Another example, this time with the predictive element: Isaiah lived in the 8th century B.C.E. God's people (the nation of Judah) were being threatened by a military alliance forged between her two immediate northern neighbors, Syria and Samaria. To warn the people not to lose faith, and to assure them that God would protect them, the Lord instructed Isaiah to give one of his children a prophetic name as a living reminder of His faithfulness. As you read the account below, remember that the child's name means, "quick to the plunder, swift to the spoil" (What a name!):

> Then I went to the prophetess [his wife], and she conceived and gave birth to a son. And the LORD said to me, "Name him Maher-Shalel-Hash-Baz. Before the boy knows how to say 'My father' or 'My mother,' the wealth of Damascus and the plunder of Samaria will be carried off by the king of Assyria" (Isaiah 8:3,4).

By this, Isaiah predicted that before the child could speak coherently, the threatening alliance would be crushed by Assyria, the superpower of the time.

Turn to the pages of the New Testament for another vantage point on prophecy. There was a gathering of believers in Y'shua (the Jewish name for Jesus) in the Greek city of Corinth during the first century of this era. They were confused about prophecy and prophesying, and since the apostle Paul had founded the group he was quick to straighten them out. He explained:

> Everyone who prophesies speaks to men for their strengthening, encouragement and comfort (1 Corinthians 14:3).

God wanted to strengthen His people by speaking through men and women. He wanted followers who had the courage of their convictions. That courage flowed more naturally as people saw God at work in their day-to-day lives.

He also wanted to encourage them because in most cases, these believers had to pay a price to follow Y'shua. Sometimes they were alienated by their families; sometimes they lost their jobs; sometimes they were persecuted by Roman authorities for treason because they called Y'shua, not Caesar, Lord. God knew they had paid a price and He wanted them to know His comforting presence.

Whenever a predictive prophecy was given, even when it was a warning of impending disaster, it was always, always, always in a message meant to guide, strengthen, encourage, or comfort God's people in their present situation.

That removes biblical prophecy from the realm of the dark saying.

God meant it all to be understood — clearly — or it would have lost its value to Him as a help for His people.

IT WASN'T WRITTEN TO YOU

The second thing you need to know about biblical prophecy is that it wasn't written to you.

That may sound elementary, but you'd be surprised at the number of people who open the Bible and read their names on every page. The truth of the matter is, God directed those messages to specific people who had specific concerns in specific situations in history. He spoke to them about things that mattered to them.

Those messages, both present and predictive, were not written to or about Westerners living in the final years of the 20th century.

However, while they weren't written to us, they were written *for* us (inasmuch as God intended them to be passed down to us and millions of others throughout time).

Let me be plain on this point. The biblical prophecies regarding the second coming of Y'shua the Messiah to earth are not about the 20th century. They are about the second coming of Y'shua the Messiah to earth. No one knows when that event will take place. I believe it will occur in our lifetime, though, because predictions of what world conditions will be at the time of the Messiah's return seem to be the world conditions with which we are living today.

So, these prophecies were not written to us, but they were written for us, and I believe they will be fulfilled in our time.

EVERY TIME GOD AIMS AND PULLS, HE HITS THE BULLSEYE

The third thing you need to know about biblical prophecy is that because God is its source, it is always right on target!

As I mentioned above, more than two-thirds of all the prophecy in the Bible has been fulfilled, exactly as it was predicted. The reason the fulfillment rate is not 100 percent is not because God, like Jeanne Dixon, missed a few. It is because some of the events or scenarios are yet to take place.

We can trust His Word for our future only to the extent that we have confidence in His past performance. So before we get into those yet-to-occur events, let's look at history.

Chapter 26 of the book of Ezekiel in the Jewish Scriptures contains one of the most unusual prophecies in the Bible. It is the record of God's message to the city of Tyre in about 590 B.C.E. It is unusual because instead of the normally general statements, this prophecy is detailed. With it we can expect a detailed fulfillment.

Tyre was a prosperous coastal city in what was, and still is, Lebanon. Tyre and Jerusalem had their ups and downs as far as inter-city relations went. At the time of this prophecy, Jerusalem and the nation of Judah had been conquered by the Babylonians, so her position as a rival to Tyre had declined dramatically. Tyre was still flourishing while Jerusalem was languishing. Keep that in mind as you read the prophecy (I have inserted numbers in the text to help you keep track of the details):

In the eleventh year, on the first day of the month, the word of the LORD came to me: "Son of man, because Tyre has said of Jerusalem, 'Aha! The gate to the nations is broken, and its doors have swung open to me; now that she lies in ruins I will prosper,' therefore this is what the Sovereign LORD says: I am against you, O Tyre, and (1) I will bring many nations against you, like the sea casting up its waves. (2) They will destroy the walls of Tyre and pull down her towers; (3) I will scrape away her rubble and make her a bare rock. (4) Out in the sea she will become a place to spread fishnets, for I have spoken, declares the Sovereign LORD. (5) She will become plunder for the nations, and her settlements on the mainland will be ravaged by the sword. Then they will know that I am the LORD.

For this is what the Sovereign LORD says: (6) From the north I am going to bring against Tyre Nebuchadnezzar king of Babylon, king of kings . . . with horsemen and a great army.

. . . (7) I will make you a bare rock, and you will become a place to spread fishnets. You will never be rebuilt, for I the LORD have spoken, declares the Sovereign LORD (Ezekiel 26:1-7,14).

Let's list those specific prophecies again:

1. Many nations will come against Tyre.

2. The walls and defensive towers will be reduced to rubble.

3. The rubble will be removed to the bare rock.

4. Tyre will survive only as a colony of fishermen, offshore.

5. Many will plunder her riches.

6. The instrument of her destruction will be Nebuchadnezzar, the Babylonian king and warlord.

7. The city will never be rebuilt.

As predictions go, that's pretty specific! None of this hazy, "I-see-trouble-in-the-future-for-Tyre" business.

The question is, did the specific predictions come to pass?

Here's how history shook it out: In 585 B.C.E., three to five years after the prophecy was delivered, Nebuchadnezzar laid siege to the city. Thirteen years later, Tyre fell. When Nebuchadnezzar broke in the gates, he found the city almost empty. The people had moved clandestinely by ships to an island a mile offshore where they had fortified a new city.

In 573 B.C.E., the year the siege ended, Nebuchadnezzar ordered the razing of the abandoned city to the ground. Not one stone was to remain on another. That fulfills predictions 2, 4 and 6 above.

The island Tyre remained a powerful city for several hundred years, during which time they had skirmishes with other nations, most notably with the Greeks under Alexander the Great. Two hundred and forty years after Nebuchadnezzar, Alexander came against the island city. Since he had no ships, he directed his engineers to demolish the old city and, by dumping the rubble into the sea, build a causeway, 200 feet wide, to the island. The site of the old city was stripped to the bedrock.

He had much trouble completing the causeway since he had no naval support, so he pressured his conquered subjects to contribute vessels to the cause. Sidon, Aradus, Byblus, Rhodes, Sli, Mallos, Lycia, Macedon and Cyprus sent ships.

After a siege of seven months, the city fell. Alexander killed 80,000 of the inhabitants and sold 30,000 into slavery. That fulfills 1, 3 and 5 above.[2]

"But what about number 7?" you ask. "Tyre still exists today, so this prophecy wasn't fulfilled 100 percent."

Good observation! However, modern Tyre is not on the site of the ancient city. It actually is a new city which took its name from the old. Old Tyre, the one whose elders Ezekiel addressed, is nothing today but a bare rock, still used by fishermen to spread their nets to dry (which, you'll recall, was predicted too).

The Bible can be trusted. It speaks as God's Word, with God's authority. We'll look at some even more convincing evidence in the next chapter.

*He is the catalyst who will change
the current order of history
into a truly new order.*

---

7. THE MORE SURE WORD OF PROPHECY IN JESUS

While Lovelle Williams would be the first to tell you that she has no idea exactly how prophetic events will play themselves out, her view of the future is, nonetheless, very clear. That is because her belief and hope for the future are centered not on a series of predicted events, but on a predicted person—Jesus, Y'shua, the Messiah.

To people who believe as Lovelle does, the events that surround the coming of this Predicted One are secondary. They are like the leaves that change in the fall: When the leaves turn brown and drift away, you know that winter is almost here. In fact, when Jesus Himself spoke of His return to the earth, He used a similar analogy:

> Now learn this lesson from the fig tree: As soon as
> its twigs get tender and its leaves come out, you know
> that summer is near. Even so, when you see all these

things [events Jesus mentioned], you know that it is near, right at the door (Matthew 24:32,33).

The events on which we will focus extensively are merely sprouts on the tips of the branches—harbingers of the inexorable change of the seasons. They are not the force behind that change.

That force is Jesus, the Messiah promised by God. He is the catalyst who will change the current order of history into a truly new order—one which He personally will oversee. But what do the prophecies say of this Messiah?

THE NATURE OF MESSIANIC PROPHECY

Just for a minute, imagine yourself as a parent of young teens. You are riding the roller coaster of joy and frustration as you see them transition from childhood into adolescence, all the time wanting them to enjoy rich, meaningful lives.

Because you know what they are going through and what lies ahead on the road to adulthood, you can help them cope with the sometimes tumultuous events and emotions you know they will encounter.

You do that by helping them gain a perspective on what is coming next in their lives, what they can expect at each stage, and by assuring them of your presence and support. To a son you might say, "You know, in junior high, boys have more energy and hostility than they have common sense. You'll find that some guys will pick at you and beg for a fight. Remember who you are. And remember I'll always support you." Or to a daughter, "Sweetheart, we're leaving for the weekend. While we're gone you will be strongly tempted to do things that we have taught you not to do; it's natural at your age. Just remember, we will be home in 48 hours."

What you tell your children about the things you know their future holds is communicated in the context of their relationship with you. A good parent is the rock that provides a sense of reference when the way gets tough.

That's the essence of messianic prophecy in the Bible.

God, the Father, knowing what was true about His children's future, always spoke in the context of their relationship with Him. And His word to us is "sure" not only because God knows all things and does not lie—but also because God spoke to us in an intimate way, in the person of the Messiah.

The whole of what God has to say to us is epitomized in one word—Jesus.

The first four books of the New Testament tell about Jesus, and each of the four presents a little different view of His life and ministry. The fourth one, the Gospel of John, gives the most insight into His unique nature:

> In the beginning was the Word, and the Word was with God, and the Word was God. He was with God in the beginning. . . . The Word became flesh and made his dwelling among us (John 1:1,2,14).

If the Bible is true and if John was correct about the nature of the Messiah (and I believe it is and he was), then prophecy that points to the Messiah not only is our Father telling His children what He knows to be true about their future—but it is also our Father promising to be physically present with them in that future!

THE PROPHECIES OF HIS COMING

Of necessity, God's message of comfort began early. Though the magnitude of the atrocities against the Jewish people by the Nazis of the Hitler era have dominated much of 20th century thought, severe persecution is hardly unique in Jewish history.

The first atrocities suffered by the Jewish people came about 3800 years ago. A colony of Jews was prospering in the fertile land of Goshen in Egypt when a new Pharaoh came to power. En masse, the Jews were stripped of their property and wealth and were made slaves of the state.

From that century to this, the Jews as a people have endured one persecution after another, one occupation after another and one oppression after another. As God's chosen people, they also became Satan's "chosen" people, that is, the target of his destructive activity designed to undercut God.

Although the Jewish people endured phenomenal hardships as the people in whom God had invested His law and revelation, they also received a wonderful privilege. God promised a Messiah, a Savior, a Deliverer. Over the 1500 years between the books of Moses and the birth of Jesus, no fewer than 61 major prophecies, with at least 300 specific details, were pronounced regarding His coming.

By laying out specific parameters of identification, one piece at a time, God invested His people, the Jews, with a complete and accurate picture of the Messiah they were to expect. When one came on the scene claiming to be sent from God and matching those credentials, His people were to acknowledge Him as their Deliverer.

Following is a complete list of all 61 of the major messianic prophecies of the Jewish Scripture, and their fulfillments. You be the judge as to whether these identifiers are adequate for their intended purpose:

THE 61 PROPHECIES OF THE OLD TESTAMENT
AND THEIR FULFILLMENT[1]

PROPHECY	SOURCE	FULFILLMENT
1. Born of the seed of woman	Genesis 3:15	Galatians 4:4
2. Born of a virgin	Isaiah 7:14	Matthew 1:18,24,25
3. Son of God	Psalm 2:7	Matthew 3:17
4. Seed of Abraham	Genesis 22:18	Matthew 1:1
5. Son of Isaac	Genesis 21:12	Luke 3:23,34
6. Son of Jacob	Numbers 24:17	Luke 3:23,34
7. Tribe of Judah	Genesis 49:10	Luke 3:23,33
8. Family line of Jesse	Isaiah 11:1	Luke 3:23,32
9. House of David	Jeremiah 23:5	Luke 3:23,31
10. Born at Bethlehem	Micah 5:2	Matthew 2:1
11. Presented with gifts	Psalm 72:10	Matthew 2:1,11
12. Herod kills children	Jeremiah 31:15	Matthew 2:16
13. Jesus' pre-existence	Micah 5:2	Colossians 1:17
14. He shall be called Lord	Psalm 110:1	Luke 20:41-44
15. Shall be Immanuel (God with us)	Isaiah 7:14	Matthew 1:23
16. Shall be a prophet	Deut. 18:18	Matthew 21:11
17. Priest	Psalm 110:4	Hebrews 5:5,6
18. Judge	Isaiah 33:22	John 5:30
19. King	Psalm 2:6	Matthew 27:37
20. Anointed of Holy Spirit	Isaiah 11:2	Matthew 3:16,17
21. His zeal for God	Psalm 69:9	John 2:15-17
22. Preceded by a messenger	Isaiah 40:3	Matthew 3:1,2

23. Ministry to begin in Galilee	Isaiah 9:1	Matthew 4:12,13
24. Ministry of miracles	Isaiah 35:5,6	Matthew 9:35
25. Teacher of parables	Psalm 78:2	Matthew 13:34
26. To enter the Temple	Malachi 3:1	Matthew 21:12
27. Enter Jerusalem on a donkey	Zechariah 9:9	Luke 19:35-37
28. "Stumbling Stone" to Jews	Psalm 118:22	1 Peter 2:7
29. Light to Gentiles	Isaiah 60:3	Acts 13:47,48
30. Resurrection	Psalm 16:10	Acts 2:31
31. Ascension	Psalm 68:18	Acts 1:9
32. Seated at right hand of God	Psalm 110:1	Hebrews 1:3
33. Betrayed by a friend	Psalm 41:9	Matthew 10:4
34. Sold for 30 pieces of silver	Zechariah 11:12	Matthew 26:15
35. That money to be thrown in God's house	Zechariah 11:13	Matthew 27:5
36. That money given to buy a potter's field	Zechariah 11:13	Matthew 27:7
37. Forsaken by followers	Zechariah 13:7	Mark 14:50
38. Accused by false witnesses	Psalm 35:11	Matthew 25:59-61
39. Silent before accusers	Isaiah 53:7	Matthew 27:12-19
40. Wounded and bruised	Isaiah 53:5	Matthew 27:26
41. Smitten and spit upon	Isaiah 50:6	Matthew 26:67
42. Mocked	Psalm 22:7,8	Matthew 27:31
43. Fell under cross	Psalm 109:24	Luke 23:26

44. Hands and feet pierced	Psalm 22:16	Luke 23:33
45. Crucified with thieves	Isaiah 53:12	Matthew 27:38
46. Prayed for persecutors	Isaiah 53:12	Luke 23:34
47. Rejected by His own people	Isaiah 53:3	John 7:5,48
48. Hated without cause	Psalm 69:4	John 15:25
49. Friends stood afar off	Psalm 38:11	Luke 23:49
50. People shook their heads	Psalm 109:25	Matthew 27:39
51. Stared upon	Psalm 22:17	Luke 23:35
52. Garments parted and lots cast for them	Psalm 22:18	John 19:23,24
53. To suffer thirst	Psalm 69:21	John 19:28
54. Gall and vinegar offered	Psalm 69:21	Matthew 27:34
55. His forsaken cry	Psalm 22:1	Matthew 27:46
56. Committed Himself to God	Psalm 31:5	Luke 23:46
57. Bones not broken	Psalm 34:20	John 19:33
58. Heart broken	Psalm 22:14	John 19:34
59. His side pierced	Zechariah 12:10	John 19:34
60. Darkness over the land	Amos 8:9	Matthew 27:45
61. Buried in rich man's tomb	Isaiah 53:9	Matthew 27:57-60

As you read through that list, you'll notice that there would be different ways to organize the prophecies so they would be easier to comprehend. You might group them as to: (1) those in which Jesus acts; and (2) those in which He is acted upon. Or you might group them according to those which speak of His suffering as opposed to those which speak of His triumphant reign.

For our purposes, let's divide them into: (1) those things over which Jesus had control (entering Jerusalem on a donkey, for example); and (2) those things over which He had no control (such as being born as a descendant of Abraham).

Someone aware of these prophecies could have been rightfully suspicious of someone who claimed to be Messiah and yet fulfilled only the predictions in the former category. So let's begin with four of the predictions from the latter category — prophecies which no human could fulfill through his own volition — and do some further investigation.

BORN OF A VIRGIN

Some prophecies predict a specific event which can have but one fulfillment, for example, the prediction of the destruction of Tyre in Ezekiel 26.

Some prophecies are more complex. Let me give you an illustration of what I mean.

I live in the state of California. If there is one thing that California is known for, it is earthquakes. Scientists and psychics alike have been predicting the "Big One" for many years, and those predictions warn us that there will be great havoc and extensive damage.

In October of 1989, a 7.1 earthquake jolted Northern California. Now, that was big enough for me, and in a sense the chaos and destruction did fulfill much of the predictions. Yet we have heard that that earthquake was only a harbinger of the "Big One" yet to come.

Biblical prophecy is sometimes like that. The promised signs can be directed at a situation in the immediate future of the prophet and the people, yet find a greater, final consummation at a later date.

This prophecy is one of those.

Writing in the eighth century B.C.E., the prophet Isaiah made this prediction:

> Therefore the Lord Himself will give you a sign: The virgin will be with child and will give birth to a son, and will call him Immanuel (Isaiah 7:14).

Like many other prophecies, this one contains two layers of meaning. The first layer referred to what was then the current historical situation. In the preceding chapter (Isaiah 6) Judah was being threatened by a military alliance between her two immediate northern neighbors, a situation which was causing more than a little consternation in the palace.

God sent the prophet to reassure King Ahaz that He was in control, and that He would not allow the alliance to triumph over Judah. "The sovereign LORD says: It will not take place, it will not happen . . . If you do not stand firm in your faith, you will not stand at all" (Isaiah 7:7,9).

To assuage the king's troubled mind even further, the Lord continued to speak through Isaiah saying, "Ask the LORD your God for a sign."

God offered a sign because He wanted to reassure Ahaz, and through Him, the people of Judah. But the distraught king behaved as though the prophet was setting a trap instead of making a bonafide offer and protested, "I will not put the LORD to the test" (verse 12).

That's when Isaiah delivered the message printed above. If Ahaz wouldn't ask for a sign of God's protection from the alliance, God would give him one anyway.

The sign was that a child would be born to a virgin, or maiden. The young woman would name the child "God with us" (Immanuel). The presence of the child whose name was "God with us" would be a perpetual reminder to the king of God's promise of protection for His people.

The Hebrew word *almah,* which is used in this passage, literally means "a young woman of marriageable age," but in all its occurrences in the Hebrew Bible, it implies virginity. "It would be axiomatic in Hebrew society that such a woman would be a virgin."[2] Though many Bible translations today do not use the word *virgin* in this passage, the Greek translation of the Hebrew Scriptures made in the third century B.C.E. (the Septuagint) clearly demonstrates that *almah* referred to a virgin. The Jewish translators selected the Greek word, *parthenos,* as the appropriate one in this passage. *Parthenos* means virgin, quite literally, one who has not engaged in sexual intercourse.[3] There isn't any claim that any young virgin gave birth to anyone in Ahaz's time. The prophecy points to one of the young women, probably of the court, bearing a first child and giving him that prophetic name.

However, on another level this prophecy points forward to the Messiah, the one who in actual fact is God with us, not merely a child whose name reminds people of His presence. In the complete fulfillment of this prophecy in its most literal sense, He would be born, not merely of a young woman, but of a young woman who was a virgin in the true sense of the word.

Even in that regard, Jesus of Nazareth completely fulfilled the prophecy of Isaiah, uttered 700 years before. He was conceived, not by natural means, but through a miracle:

This is how the birth of Jesus Christ came about:
His mother Mary was pledged to be married to Joseph,

but before they came together [that is, had sex], she was found to be with child through the Holy Spirit.

. . . Joseph . . . took Mary home as his wife. But he had no union with her until she gave birth to a son. And he gave him the name Jesus (Matthew 1:18,24).

BORN AT BETHLEHEM

Obviously no one has control over where they are born. So, if we have a prediction of the place of Messiah's birth—an event completely beyond His control—then we have another valid authentication.

The prophet Micah was possibly a contemporary of Isaiah. Micah delivered a message different from Isaiah's, although Isaiah himself addressed the same issue on other occasions. The moral character of the nation of Judah had declined alarmingly. Thus Micah's invective:

Her leaders judge for a bribe,
   her priests teach for a price,
   and her prophets tell fortunes for money (Micah 3:11).

God's message through Micah warned that such a standard of behavior was wholly unacceptable among the people of God and would be dealt with harshly unless a change occurred. God's punishment for Judah's continued unacceptable behavior would come in the form of war. Jerusalem would be leveled—plowed under—by an invading army.

The prophecy was fulfilled just more than a century later. Yet in Micah's vision of destruction, there was hope:

But you, Bethlehem Ephrathah,
   though you are small among the clans of Judah,
out of you will come for me
   one who will be ruler over Israel,
whose origins are from of old,
   from ancient times (Micah 5:2).

Sometime between 6 and 4 B.C.E., Jesus was born in the village of Bethlehem in the Judean hills. His parents' home was Nazareth, 125 miles to the north. But in order to comply with the requirements of the Roman census, they had been forced to travel during His mother's pregnancy to their ancestral village of Bethlehem:

> In those days Caesar Augustus [the Roman Emperor] issued a decree that a census should be taken of the entire Roman world. . . . And everyone went to his own town to register. So Joseph also went up from the town of Nazareth in Galilee to Judea, to Bethlehem the town of David, because he belonged to the house and line of David. . . . While they were there, the time came for [Mary's] baby to be born, and she gave birth to her firstborn, a son (Luke 2:1-7).

In spite of the fact that they actually lived in Nazareth, Mary and Joseph had to travel to the very place which Micah had predicted would be the birthplace of the Messiah.

And there Jesus was born.

Fluke?

PRESENTED WITH GIFTS FROM ARABIA

The book of Psalms is an extensive collection of songs and poetry whose composition spans a long period of time. The oldest parts were written by David and Solomon about 1000 B.C.E. The newest were written during and after the exile in Babylon 400 years later.

The collection is divided into five sections or "Books." The first two are composed primarily of songs written by David and Solomon. The seventy-second psalm, a song by the fabulously wealthy and powerful King Solomon, was placed at the end of this most ancient section. In it, Solomon, himself a mighty monarch, sang of his King, the

Davidic descendant at whose coming Solomon's earthly regency would pale by comparison:

> He will rule from sea to sea
>   and from the River to the ends of the earth. . . .
> The kings of Tarshish and of distant shores will bring
>   tribute to him;
> the kings of Sheba and Seba
>   will present him gifts (Psalm 72:8,10).

Sheba and Seba were on the Arabian peninsula. Their inhabitants were known as Sabeans, and the Israelites referred to them as "the men of the East."

> After Jesus was born in Bethlehem in Judea, during the time of King Herod, Magi [court astrologers] from the east came to Jerusalem. . . . They [found] the child with his mother Mary, and they . . . opened their treasures and presented him with gifts of gold and of incense and of myrrh (Matthew 2:1,11).

The gifts the astrologers presented to Jesus represented the finest products of their desert kingdoms. They truly were gifts fit for a King.

Coincidence?

INFANTS KILLED IN ASSOCIATION WITH MESSIAH'S COMING

Some time near the end of the seventh century B.C.E. God delivered a grim vision to the prophet Jeremiah:

> A voice is heard in Ramah,
>   mourning and great weeping,
> Rachel weeping for her children
>   and refusing to be comforted,
>   because her children are no more (Jeremiah 31:15).

This prophecy is a bitter one. It is also very unusual because it comes in the middle of otherwise bright and hopeful pronouncements:

> I have loved you with an everlasting love (31:3).
>
> Sing with joy for Jacob (31:7).
>
> He who scatters Israel will gather them (31:10).

Jeremiah was prophesying the restoration of the people after their devastation by Babylon; and in the longer view, he was predicting the time when Messiah would come. It is a comforting and joyous proclamation — except for the shocking passage about mass infanticide.

Somehow (not even Jeremiah knew how or why) there would be tremendous grief associated with the coming of the Messiah because Jewish children would die in great numbers.

The Gospel of Matthew gives an account of how this was fulfilled. When the court astrologers came from the east, they stopped at Jerusalem first to ask where they could find the one who had been born "king of the Jews." If they wanted to establish diplomatic relations with the new regime, Jerusalem was the logical starting place.

But they hadn't counted on the presence of Herod, the existing ruler of the Jewish people. Herod the Great was literally a paranoid madman. He had no legitimate claim to the throne. The true king should have been a Jewish descendent of the tribe of Judah, which was the family line of David.

The problem was that Herod was half Jewish and half Edomite, a military man who had clawed his way to the top and ultimately had purchased the title "king of the Jews" in an intrigue that involved Antony and Cleopatra. Herod, understandably, jealously guarded his vulnerable power.

So when the magi came with news of a heavenly sign that portended the birth of the "king of the Jews," Herod was driven by fear to act decisively. He offered to aid the officials in their search for this newborn king and requested that they inform him of the child's whereabouts when they located Him.

Instead, the magi left the country through a back route after God warned them in a dream of Herod's machinations.

But Herod was not to be stopped so easily.

When he realized that he had been outwitted by the magi, he was furious, and he gave orders to kill all the male children in Bethlehem and its vicinity who were two years old and under. He chose boys of that age based on his calculations of when the magi had seen the star.

By killing them all, he was sure to get the one he wanted.

A madman? Yes! But this wasn't the only time he acted on his paranoia. During his reign he had four of his own sons executed because he feared they were plotting against him.

Herod's cruelty was truly incredible—but the fact remains that this tragic chapter in history was a precise fulfillment of that strange and bitter prophecy of Jeremiah.

"But," one might say, "isn't it possible that the prophecy was really meant for something else, such as the Babylonian exile, and it just lines up with the birth of Jesus by coincidence?"

A good question, but the answer is no. We know from Jeremiah's own words (the context of this prophecy) that he clearly was referring to a new age, not just the return of exiles. He was careful to identify the time:

"The time is coming," says the LORD,
  "when I will make a new covenant
with the house of Israel . . .
It will not be like the covenant
  I made with their forefathers
when I took them . . . out of Egypt [referring to the
Exodus and the covenant of the law with Moses — the
central events of Judaism].
  " . . . after that time," declares the LORD,
"I will put my law in their minds
  and write it on their hearts" (Jeremiah 31:31-33).

This new era was not merely the return of the captives
from exile. It was the start of a new chapter in which the
Messiah would be the main character.

JESUS, THE MESSIAH — FULFILLMENT OF THE PROPHECIES

To appreciate the astonishing accuracy of biblical
prophecy and its actualization in history in one single
individual, you have to realize that EVERY SINGLE ONE
OF THE 61 PROPHECIES REGARDING THE COMING
OF MESSIAH WAS FULFILLED IN JESUS OF
NAZARETH.

Just a coincidence? Consider this. In 1963, Peter
Stoner selected eight of the 61 prophecies listed above and
projected the probability that any one human being might
have fulfilled all eight. (All of his selections were from the
"no control" category we set out above — the fulfillment of
which no human could have control.)

His conclusions were reviewed by H. Harold Hartzler
of the American Scientific Affiliation. Professor Hartzler
concluded:

    The manuscript [of Stoner's work] . . . has been
found, in general, to be dependable and accurate in
regard to the scientific material presented. The mathe-

matical analysis included is based upon principles of probability which are thoroughly sound, and Professor Stoner has applied these principles in a proper and convincing way.[4]

Stoner concluded that "the chance that any man might have lived down to the present time and fulfilled all eight prophecies is 1 in 10 to the 17th power."[5] That is one chance in 100,000,000,000,000,000!

To help his reader grasp the enormity of such an event occurring by coincidence, Stoner illustrated:

> Suppose we take 10 to the 17th in silver dollars and lay them on the face of Texas. They will cover all of the state two feet deep. Now mark one of these silver dollars and stir the whole mass thoroughly, all over the state.
>
> Blindfold a man and tell him that he can travel as far as he wishes, but he must pick up one silver dollar and say that this is the right one. What chance would he have of getting the right one? Just the same chance that the prophets would have had of writing these eight prophecies and having them all come true in any one man.[6]

It's true that if you searched hard enough, you could find someone who might fulfill one or two of the "no control" category and a few of the others. For someone to fulfill only eight of the "no control" category would be a mind-boggling task.

But Jesus of Nazareth fulfilled EVERY SINGLE ONE OF THE 61 PROPHECIES!

That leads us to two simple conclusions:

1. The prophecy in the Word of God is completely trustworthy—literally a "more sure word of prophecy"; and,

2. Jesus is who He claimed to be.

*Even those who denounce Jesus
as a false Messiah are witnesses
on His behalf. Why?*

8. THE HOSTILE WITNESS

One final note about the authenticity of Scripture. You might expect me, as a believer in Y'shua (Jesus), to present a strong and direct case for the Bible. In fact, you'd probably be surprised if I did not.

You're right. I do want to interest you in seeing what the Bible says. But if you are trying to judge whether or not Jesus is the Messiah, mine is not going to be the most persuasive voice. Another "testimony," one from a sometimes willing, sometimes angry, witness, should be heard before the jury goes into deliberations.

JUDGE WAPNER

When it comes to witnesses, I learned an important lesson from Judge Wapner. Yes, that's right. The famous Judge Wapner who settles things so expeditiously on *People's Court*. I met him long before he was a TV star.

The occasion of our meeting was a traffic ticket; I received a citation for running a stop sign. I've had traffic tickets for going too slow, but in my many decades of driving it was the first time I had failed to stop at a stop sign.

After the officer wrote up my ticket, my passenger and I circled back to check out the intersection at which the alleged violation had taken place.

Lo and behold! The stop sign was obscured by banana trees.

I went home, got out my Polaroid camera, and returned to the site to take two or three photos of the intersection and those lovely trees. My passenger, a friend who was a graphic artist by profession, reconstructed the scene with graphs and charts.

I then opted for my day in court instead of a fine.

The day my case came up, I entered the courtroom armed with my Polaroids, my charts . . . and my friend. Judge Wapner glanced at my evidence and immediately dismissed the Polaroid photographs. He stated that they proved nothing, since they could have been taken at any time. He also said that they were taken from a disadvantageous angle.

Then I introduced Darwin, my passenger, as a witness. He testified that the stop sign had been obscured on the day the ticket was issued. After a couple of questions posed to ascertain if Darwin was my friend, Judge Wapner turned to me and said, "Is that all?"

"Yes, your honor," I said with a deliberate nod.

"Your photos are inadmissible, and furthermore, this fellow is your friend. He will say anything you want him to say. Guilty as charged!" he pronounced as the gavel fell. "Pay the $40 fine."

I valued my friendship with Darwin, a bond that stretched back to 1958. But at that moment, I wished he had not been my friend.

The testimony of a friendly witness carries little weight in court.

THE TESTIMONY OF ANGER

On the other hand, I am still grateful to an unfriendly witness who once testified on my behalf.

It was some forty years ago. I was a student at Northeastern Bible College and a missionary trainee with the American Board of Missions to the Jews. I was assigned to conduct outdoor meetings to preach the gospel on Sunday afternoons. My post was at 73rd and Broadway (New York City) in front of the Chase Manhattan Bank.

I did not want to do it. Had it been left to me, I never would have chosen that assignment.

Every Sunday afternoon was the same: Old regulars would gather, someone would heckle me, and by the time I finished, the crowd would swell to sixty or seventy. Over the weeks and months, I came to love it.

Then in my senior year, the situation changed.

Many people had responded positively to the message of Jesus. A number of them were Jewish. Their decisions to believe in Jesus did not go unnoticed. A few men who felt that I was posing a threat to the Jewish religion appointed themselves to do something about it. They would put a stop to my street preaching.

So the violence erupted.

One Sunday after I had finished giving my talk, another Jewish Christian named Molly Fettner was telling why she believed in Jesus. A man I had known leaned forward to say something to me. I moved toward him and leaned over so as not to interrupt Ms. Fettner.

Suddenly, strong hands grabbed me from behind and clenched fists pummeled me from the front. Almost immediately I heard a siren. A man yelled, "There he is!" to the two police officers who appeared.

Someone else yelled, "We're holding him. He punched this little guy!"

At that, a diminutive man stepped forward, holding out a pair of broken glasses.

I was being set up.

If those men could convince the police and a judge that I had assaulted this man, my reputation would be irreparably hurt and my effectiveness as a minister would be history. I was bewildered.

The two policemen cuffed me and drove me to the 20th Precinct, only a few blocks away.

Fourteen people followed us.

Fourteen people lined up at the sergeant's desk.

Fourteen people signed statements claiming that "the big guy [me] became enraged and attacked the little guy."

At least I assumed that all fourteen people had made statements. But one man had kept silent. He waited until the desk sergeant finished with the paperwork and then asked, "Sergeant, do you know who I am?"

The sergeant squinted and shook his head.

"My name is Captain Horowitz. For many years I was the commander of the 19th Precinct."

"Oh, yeah. How ya' doin', Captain?"

"Let me make my statement." He got right to the point. "I don't believe in the BLEEP nonsense this turncoat Jew preaches," he gave me a cold, icy glance. "But I want to say that I am ashamed of my people. I was at the scene the whole time. That stupid preacher didn't hit anyone. Just the opposite. These people grabbed him, nearly slugged the stuffing out of him, and made up a story about him hitting the little guy to boot."

By this time, the "eyewitnesses" were backing up, heading for the door.

"Stay put!" the sergeant ordered. "If what this man says is true, you've all committed felonies."

That day I had many hostile witnesses testifying against me, and only one speaking for me.

It only took one.

One friendly witness couldn't help me overturn a traffic ticket. One hostile witness saved me from a felony conviction, most likely a jail term, and the devastation of my ministry.

ISRAEL—THE TESTIMONY OF SURVIVAL

Every living Jew—whether a believer in the Jewish religion, or in Jesus, or in nothing at all—is evidence that the God of the Bible "is" and that He keeps His Word.

Four thousand years ago, in 2000 B.C.E., God made a simple promise to Abraham:

> I will establish my covenant as an everlasting covenant between me and you and your descendants after you for the generations to come, to be your God and the God of your descendants after you (Genesis 17:7).

Whatever became of those descendants, otherwise known as the Jewish people? There have been the 470 years of slavery in Egypt, the immense problems of forging a nation from slaves who had no experiences to prepare them for nationhood, bitter internal strife, devastating wars and a seventy-year captivity, hundreds of years of external rule and oppression, a scattering of the nation throughout the world, complete destruction of the national identity by the Romans, bitter persecution throughout two millennia, a holocaust, and a modern homeland surrounded by forces pledged to their destruction.

They are 4000 years of the most extraordinary pressure ever experienced by any unified group in history.

Yet the Jewish people are still alive today, just as God promised Abraham. By our very survival, we are a testimony to the faithfulness of God.

Maybe you don't believe in spiritual forces of evil who oppose God. But if there were such a being as Satan, and if he had been able to destroy the Jewish people at some point during the endless centuries of trouble, he would have succeeded in negating God's promise, thereby invalidating the trustworthiness of God's Word.

That did not happen.

Whether you believe that attempts to wipe out the Jewish people were backed by a malevolent spiritual being or just man's own inhumanity to man, the fact remains, we have survived against all odds.

To this, the Jewish people are willing witnesses. Many freely give God the credit for our survival as a people.

ISRAEL—THE HOSTILE WITNESS

However, when it comes to Jesus, most Jewish people are, without realizing it, hostile witnesses.

God made this thriving people, His ancient people, a repository for His Word and intended that we be His messengers. Yet when the Word became flesh, that is, when God came to earth in the person of the Messiah, Jesus of Nazareth, many of His own people rejected Him:

> He was in the world, and though the world was made through him, the world did not recognize him. He came to that which was his own, but his own did not receive him (John 1:10,11).

Jesus (Y'shua) was born a Jew. He came to His own people, and while thousands of Jewish individuals saw and accepted Him, the majority did not.

Yet, out of the fringes of the crowd looking on in history, a multitude of people, formerly hostile to Judaism, have stepped forth and embraced that which Israel rejected. Millions upon millions of Gentiles have accepted Jesus as the Messiah—the one promised to Israel, not to them. Millions upon millions of people who had no connection whatsoever to the God of the Bible—who had not one drop of the blood of Abraham in their veins, and who had no part whatsoever in the ethnic tradition of the Holy Scripture—accepted the Jewish Messiah.

That is nothing short of remarkable. Had the Jewish people as a whole accepted Jesus, the world could have said, with justification, "Yes, that is because of your culture and your tradition."

This phenomenon demonstrates in another way that God and His Word are trustworthy.

But let me make one thing clear: This trustworthiness is not based on whether Jews accept or reject His work in history any more than it is based on whether Gentiles accept or reject it. God and His Word are trustworthy because He is God and it is His Word. Nothing else is needed.

A WITNESS NONETHELESS

The irony of the survival of the Jewish people and our existence in the modern world is that it hinges on a rather one-sided faithfulness. It is not the faithfulness of Israel in serving the Lord. It is the faithfulness of the Lord in keeping His Word.

That is not to say that the people of Israel have been more sinful than any other people. It's just that with the activity of God in our midst and His promise of blessings and judgments, we should have been more faithful.

God's love for Israel has been everlasting (Jeremiah 31:3), but the Hebrew Scriptures record that oftentimes that love was unrequited:

> When Israel was a child, I loved him, and out of Egypt I called my son. But the more I called Israel, the further they went from me. They sacrificed to the Baals and they burned incense to images. It was I who taught Ephraim to walk, taking them by the arms; but they did not realize it was I who healed them. I led them with cords of human kindness, with ties of love; I lifted the yoke from their neck and bent down to feed them (Hosea 11:1-4).

Even today, thousands of years after Hosea, most Jewish people are unaware of our relationship with God. The Jewish Bible, the very book that testifies of God's love for Israel, is rarely read by the average Jewish person!

Jesus made a bold remark when He said, "If you believed Moses, you would believe me, for he wrote about me" (John 5:46). God kept His commitment to the Jewish people, not only by assuring our survival, but also by sending Jesus as the Messiah.

So ready or not, willing or not, the survival of the Jewish people into the modern age demonstrates the existence of God—and because of that survival, God's Word is verified as trustworthy.

It is that very Word which speaks of the Messiah. So if, by our existence, the Jewish people testify to the truthfulness of God and the Scriptures, then even those who denounce Jesus as a false Messiah are witnesses on His behalf. Why? Because, as we saw in the last chapter, the same Scriptures which point to the survival of the Jewish people point to Jesus.

GOD'S CHOOSING

A Jewish comedian creates this scene, where the Almighty is receiving a delegation of Jews from earth. The spokesman of the delegation steps up to the creator and confronts Him with: "Is it true that the Jews are God's chosen people?"

"Yes!" booms the voice of the Almighty. "I have chosen you."

"Well," counters the spokesman, "why don't You choose someone else for a while?"

Chosenness, a call to holiness and exemplary life as a nation, is not a mantle that my Jewish people have worn comfortably. Today it is popular to reverse that mantle so it can be worn more easily. There are those who say, "We Jews are not the 'chosen people' but the 'choosing people.' We have chosen God; we have chosen to serve Him." Though that sounds reasonable and would be comforting to believe, I don't think it is accurate. I don't think we chose God. I do think God chose us. And I think He is waiting for us to respond.

Because of my faith in Jesus, many of my fellow Jews regard me as an ex-Jew, so I am hardly considered a spokesman for the Jewish community. But I want it known that regardless of how the rest of the Jewish community chooses to view those of us Jews who believe in Jesus, we still regard ourselves as Jews.

Further, we regard the Jewish people as a whole as having been set aside by God — chosen — for a definite purpose.

It's true that some Jewish people view the concept of "the chosen" as little more than a sad joke. Many of us have been unwilling to accept that title. It is difficult for most to imagine what God has chosen us for, other than to suffer. If that were the case, it is understandable that, like the fellow at the gates of heaven in the joke, we might wish God would "choose" someone else for a change.

Yet if most of my people could have a real sense of what we were chosen to be or do, there would be great joy and great zeal to fulfill that destiny.

And frankly, God's purpose for us is really no mystery. It is explained in the Torah in the book of Deuteronomy:

> For you are a people holy to the LORD your God. The LORD your God has chosen you out of all the peoples on the face of the earth to be his people, his treasured possession. The LORD did not set his affection on you and choose you because you were more numerous than other peoples, for you were the fewest of all peoples. But it was because the LORD loved you and kept the oath he swore to your forefathers that he brought you out with a mighty hand and redeemed you from the land of slavery, from the power of Pharaoh king of Egypt (Deuteronomy 7:6-8).

It was not because we were a large, powerful people that God chose us. Nor was it for our intelligence, wisdom, success or good looks. No, it was because God made a promise to Abraham, Isaac and Jacob that He would raise up a special people through whom the entire world could find blessing.

Read the words God spoke to Abraham centuries before Moses was born:

> The LORD had said to Abram, "Leave your country, your people and your father's household and go to the land I will show you. I will make you into a great nation and I will bless you; I will make your name great, and you will be a blessing. I will bless those who bless you, and whoever curses you I will curse; and all peoples on earth will be blessed through you" (Genesis 12:1-3).

A MISSION, A MESSAGE

The Lord had promised that Abraham would be the ancestor of a great nation through whom the rest of humanity would be blessed: a nation with a divinely ordained mission.

Now, to tell the truth, most of my people are not at all comfortable with the word *mission*. At best we think of Spanish monks living in red-tiled mission buildings such as can be found scattered throughout California: quaint and interesting to study in the context of history, but not for us Jews.

More often the word *mission* causes us to think of those who have tortured and executed Jews for refusing to convert. This common connotation of mission and missionary is not without some basis in history.

Still, according to the Hebrew Bible, we Jews were chosen to be missionaries. Stripped of its unfavorable connotation and viewed apart from those who have twisted its application, the concept of mission should not make us cringe. To have a mission simply means to have a message and an obligation to share that message with others.

What is the Jewish mission? It was and is to make God known to the rest of the world:

> Now if you obey me fully and keep my covenant,
> then out of all nations you will be my treasured posses-
> sion. Although the whole earth is mine, you will be for
> me a kingdom of priests and a holy nation (Exodus
> 19:5,6).

In biblical times, a priest was one who represented God to the people. God intended the Jewish people to be a nation of priests for Him. In order to fulfill that role, we had to obey God fully and keep His covenant. I don't think there is or has been a rabbi who could say that, as a people, we have managed to do that. (In fairness, there aren't any other nations who have done so, either.)

How can we understand what it means to be chosen by God if we no longer truly understand who God is or what He requires of us? The concept of mission is rejected largely because it is presumed that anyone claiming to have a message from God is self-aggrandizing and pushing his or her own opinion onto others in the name of religion.

In reality, that presumption really says something about what we think of God—that we can't really know anything about Him for certain. But if the Bible is true, and God has some way in particular for us to know Him, it would be more self-aggrandizing to excuse ourselves from delivering His message on the grounds that it would be disrespectful to those who have their own religion.

If there is a God who has a message, then we should be in awe of our calling to deliver that message. The problem is, we cannot transmit a message that we have not received for ourselves.

Some Jewish people believe in God while others do not. Among those who do believe, there are varying concepts of who God is and how much He is, or should be, involved in our day-to-day lives. We have no agreed-upon message to take to the nations. Yet God has kept His promises by keeping us alive as a nation. Even if we haven't always been spiritually minded, the world has still been blessed by the Jewish people in partial fulfillment of the promise to Abraham.

Even in a day when many of us have abandoned faith in God, our people still furnish society with a disproportionately large number of doctors, teachers and lawyers. And the Hebrew Scriptures, faithfully transmitted by generations of Jewish scribes, remain accessible to the world.

Those Jewish people who, for all practical purposes, have forgotten God still retain a glimmer of the ancient vision for Him. It is a vision planted by the Almighty Himself.

*Five predictions about Israel
in the last days.*

---

9. THE MIDDLE EAST TODAY — HOW DID WE GET TO WHERE WE ARE?

ISRAEL

For 3800 years, the Jewish people have clung to the promise God made to Abraham. Through all kinds of persecution the Jewish soul has flourished because of the awareness, which is sometimes subconscious, that God has designated a "place" for us.

Jews like Tessie Ginsberg will give up time and money to ensure that the promise of a place, our place, will be realized. Israeli citizens will pay gladly with their lives to protect their descendents' rights to that promised land.

The belief that modern Jews should have a secure territory in our ancient homeland is called Zionism. But Zionism is more than that. Even for the Diaspora, Jewish identity is shaped in large part by the affirmation that Israel is a Jewish state—a place belonging not only to its citizens, but a state and a land belonging to all Jews everywhere.

Zionism is rooted in God's ancient promises to Abraham. God promised Abraham more than a nation of descendants. He promised a land.

Oh, there are people who don't like Jews and who ascribe negative meaning to the term "Zionist." They want reasons to affirm their dislikes, so they theorize about supposed Jewish conspiracies and label anything Jewish as the "Israel lobby" or "Zionist propaganda."

These are people whose grandparents actually convinced themselves that "the Jews" controlled the economic infrastructure of the world.

But the Zionist dream was never remotely connected with ambitions for a world takeover. It was and is the aspiration that arose in the hearts and minds of people who could never sever their ties to their fellow Jews.

PEOPLE OF THE PROMISE, PEOPLE OF THE LAND

The Jewish longing for a homeland stretches back to the early years of the second century C.E. when the Roman legions put a final end to Israel as a nation in the ancient world.

The modern movement to re-establish that homeland dates to the 1800s. Theodore Herzl launched a political movement, which he dubbed "Zionism, based on a secular ideology." His dream was to institute a Jewish state in the region of Palestine.

This secular movement forced an historic break with religious messianism, which held that there could be no Jewish homeland until the Messiah came to regather the Jewish people to the ancient land of promise. The Zionist movement harnessed the yearning for the land and shaped it into a potent political force.

In the latter decades of the 19th century, the world political climate was ripe for this movement. Educated European Jews had high hopes for liberalization of conditions in Russia, and the future looked bright.

Then came the virulent anti-Semitic pogroms (organized persecutions) that began in 1881.

The Jewish response was mixed. More than two and a half million eastern European Jews emigrated to the West. Those who remained "were influenced by nationalist ferment that was rife throughout Europe. The nation, rather than the individual, was increasingly regarded as the proper subject of self-determination."[1]

In that setting, Leon Pinsker, a leader in the movement and the author of the immensely popular and influential pamphlet, "Autoemancipation," put forth a powerful argument: The dignity of the Jewish people could be sustained in the modern world only if Jews lived in their own territory as a self-governing nation, as did other peoples.

Pinsker's proposal stimulated a movement within the movement (Hovevei Zion—Lovers of Zion) which encouraged Jews to settle in Palestine. By the end of the century, 24,000 settlers had arrived, rapidly doubling the Jewish population there.

But the "practical Zionists," as the early pioneers were called, failed. They were unable to develop a sound economic base and had to depend on the largesse of Baron Edmund de Rothschild of France to ward off disaster.

NOT AT ALL QUIET ON THE WESTERN FRONT

Meanwhile in western Europe, Herzl was unimpressed by the failed efforts of the eastern European Jews in Palestine. He agreed with Pinsker, but insisted that the only magnet capable of attracting mass immigration to the Jewish state was full recognition of a legitimate, independent Jewish nation by the leading powers of the world.

To that end he established the World Zionist Organization in 1897.

At first, Herzl didn't believe it was necessary for the Jewish state to be in Palestine. Russian Jews, however, ultimately persuaded him that the only physical location which would inspire worldwide Jewish support was the land of God's ancient promise.

As the fledgling movement gained momentum, it also gained internal strife. Religious, cultural and labor factions all strove for leadership within the Zionist cause, each with its own vision of the future. Ultimately, the labor Zionists, headed by Chaim Weizmann in the diplomatic arena and David Ben-Gurion in Palestine, captured the imagination of the movement.

During World War I, Weizmann convinced the British that an alliance with the Jews would advance their war aims and their imperial interests in the Middle East. In 1917, an important diplomatic coup took place: the Balfour Declaration, promising British protection for Zionist development in Palestine.

That milestone declaration was a letter dated November 2, 1917, addressed to Lord Rothschild. In that letter Balfour made a commitment to the Zionist cause on behalf of his government:

Dear Lord Rothschild,

I have much pleasure in conveying to you, on behalf of His Majesty's Government, the following declaration of sympathy with Jewish Zionist aspirations, which has been submitted to, and approved by, the Cabinet.

"His Majesty's government view with favour the establishment in Palestine of a national home for the Jewish people, and will use their best endeavors to facilitate the achievement of this object, it being clearly understood that nothing shall be done which may prejudice the civil and religious rights of existing non-Jewish communities in Palestine or the rights and political status enjoyed by Jews in any other country."

I should be grateful if you would bring this declaration to the knowledge of the Zionist Federation.

Yours sincerely,

Arthur James Balfour.[2]

While this was a private letter, it did put the British government on record as supporting Zionism and in addition gave focus to the movement. While there were many who had wanted to see a homeland for the Jewish people, they were still considering such places as Africa, Madagascar or South America. Balfour's letter ended any speculation about where to establish Jewish colonies once and for all.

An almost mystical consensus united Jewish hearts around the world with the hope of a Jewish homeland in the land of ancient promise.

THE MANDATE AT LAST IS GIVEN

On April 25, 1920, the Supreme Council of the Peace Conference accepted the Balfour Declaration and the Palestine Mandate was established at San Remo.

Jewish people all over the world celebrated!

San Remo, a little town on the Italian Riviera, was one of thirty-three international conference sites. What set it apart was that at this conference, an historic turning point was reached—the Allies at last agreed they were "in favor of the establishment in Palestine of a national home for the Jewish people."

Almost immediately, global forces began to mitigate against the dream-come-true. The British and French were feeling tremors on the geopolitical landscape. The Bolsheviks had risen to power in Russia as the Czarist regime collapsed. Turkey, the head of the Ottoman Empire—of which Israel was a former colony—was needed as a buffer against Russian communism.

In another arena, the British and French monopolized Middle East oil supplies by leveraging their influence as colonial powers. In return, the Arabs' oil agreements gave them influence with the Europeans which they used to resist the realization of the Zionist dream of a homeland in Israel.

NEVER SAY DIE

Twenty years later, in the face of insignificant Jewish immigration to Palestine and increasing Arab opposition (strikes and riots) to its policy, Britain ordered the Peel Commission. Officially called the Royal Commission on Palestine and under the leadership of Earl Peel, the commission was to study the explosive situation and make recommendations to the British government.

In July of 1937 the Commission concluded that the Zionist Mandate was unworkable, and they recommended partition of the land between Arabs and Jews. In an accompanying document, the British government accepted this partition in principle, but did not actually follow through on the recommendation.

That proved to be a turning point for Zionism. It was a movement deeply divided, but its leaders acquiesced to the British because Weizmann and Ben-Gurion successfully argued that a strong alliance with a powerful Britain was too valuable to endanger.

At the same time, Hitler was beginning his slaughter of European Jews, instilling tremendous fear throughout world Jewry. More than ever it became obvious that a Jewish state was the only way to ensure Jewish survival.

Zionism enjoyed soaring support among Jews. The sense of impending disaster brought the backing of Jews in the West, who remained skeptical of Zionism's ideology while accepting its conclusions.

The Yishuv, Zionists already living in the land, became the center of the movement and began to harness the resources of their worldwide network in a rush toward establishing statehood.

The swelling ranks of pioneers could not endure the thought of living as a mere community under the rule of outsiders.

Immediately following World War II, in the wake of the tragedy of the Holocaust, Ben-Gurion assumed the mantle of leadership. American Jewry became his chief ally.

In the years between 1936 and 1948, the international image of the Yishuv changed from one of Jewish powerlessness, well-meaning people in a more-or-less losing struggle, into Jewish sovereignty, a vibrant and well-organized entity which was effecting change for the good.

The United Nations, in May of 1948, recognized Israel as an independent nation.

The gates of immigration were opened and a river of refugees from Europe and a flood of Jews from the Arab lands poured into Israel. New political allegiances were formed and the many factions drew together to make the new nation firm.

The net effect of these sweeping events?

"For the secularist majority, the community of belongers rather than believers, Zionism generated a new way of being Jewish in order to survive."[3]

A PROMISED LAND—BUT NOT AN EDEN

Since 1948, Jewish people the world over have regarded Eretz Yisrael (the land of Israel) as a commanding symbol of our identity. It embodies our long history, cultural diversity and unifying traditions.

For modern Israeli citizens, though, there is a high price to pay for being part of a nation born in conflict, an ante that was upped by the actions of Saddam Hussein in both the military and the media. In an *Esquire* magazine article filed under the subtitle, "Dispatches From the Meanest Streets in the World," one reporter made these observations about the current state of affairs in Israel:

> In the fight over the land the Jews call Israel and the Arabs call Palestine, the moderate position has always been that a division of turf and power could be fashioned that would allow the two peoples to live side by side in something resembling peace. But Palestinian support for Saddam kicked the slats out from under the Jewish moderates' claim that Israel's Arabs did not really wish the destruction of the Jews; the Temple Mount killings knocked the bottom out of the Arab moderates' notion that the Palestinian uprising, or *intifada,* should be waged without resorting to arms; and the scope of the great Russian *aliyah* (the immigration expected over the next two years) made the idea that the Israelis might give up their attempts to settle the occupied territories seem ludicrous.

... Previous forms of extremism ... no longer seemed extreme enough, and new, more virulent strains appeared.[4]

Is this the Promised Land pledged to the patriarch Abraham?

Yes! At least in the prophetic vision of what the Bible calls "the last days." The prophecy regarding the last days is very clear as related to Israel, identifying several factors.

First of all, the prophecy both predicts and assumes that the descendants of Abraham will be in possession or repossession of the land. This is a very important point, because from 135 C.E. to 1948 C.E., that had not been the case. Only after 1948 was it possible for the prophecy to be fulfilled. The prophet Jeremiah had predicted a time when Israel would be regathered to the Promised Land:

> "So do not fear, O Jacob my servant;
>   do not be dismayed, O Israel," declares the LORD.
> "I will surely save you out of a distant place,
>   your descendants from the land of their exile.
> Jacob [the people] will again have peace and security,
>   and no one will make him afraid" (Jeremiah 30:10).

Second, prophecy indicates that the city of Jerusalem (and by implication its Jewish inhabitants) will be a source of major problems for the world community:

> This is the Word of the LORD concerning Israel. The LORD ... declares: "I am going to make Jerusalem a cup that sends all the surrounding peoples reeling" (Zechariah 12:1,2).

Third, a world coalition will for some reason send a military force against Jerusalem which will meet with no success:

> On that day, when all the nations of the earth are gathered against her, I will make Jerusalem an immov-

able rock for all the nations. All who try to move it will injure themselves (Zechariah 12:3).

Fourth, at some point in those stressful days, the ancient Jewish Temple will be rebuilt on the holy Temple Mount in Jerusalem. First constructed by Solomon in the mid-900s B.C.E., that Temple was destroyed by the Babylonians (now modern Iraq) under Nebuchadnezzar in 586 B.C.E. It was rebuilt by Zerubbabel in 515 B.C.E.

Herod the Great undertook a massive renovation of the Temple beginning about 20 B.C.E. which lasted for several decades. In 70 C.E., the Roman legions under Titus destroyed Jerusalem and leveled the Temple, leaving only the expansive foundation platform.

In 691 C.E., the famous mosque, Qubbet es-Sakhra (better known as the Dome of the Rock) was completed on the ancient foundation platform of the Jewish Temple. A smaller mosque, the El-Aksa mosque, was later constructed at one side of the platform. Both Muslim holy places stand to this day.

Prophecy foretells the rebuilding of the Jewish Temple and the reinstitution of the sacrifices prescribed in the Law of Moses. In a vision of the future Temple, Ezekiel received this word:

> Son of man, this is the place of my throne and the place for the soles of my feet. This is where I will live among the Israelites forever.... Describe the temple to the people of Israel, that they may be ashamed of their sins. Let them consider the plan.... Write [it] down before them so that they may be faithful to its design and follow all its regulations (Ezekiel 43:7,10,11).

Some way, somehow, the Temple will be rebuilt, in spite of the fact that two Arab shrines now stand on the only site on earth where this Temple may stand.

Fifth, at the height of that final conflict, Messiah will appear to rescue His people from certain destruction at the hands of the international coalition and initiate a period of peace:

> I will gather all the nations to Jerusalem to fight against it; the city will be captured, the houses ransacked, and the women raped. Half of the city will go into exile, but the rest of the people will not be taken from the city. Then the Lord will go out and fight against those nations (Zechariah 14:2,3).

A QUESTION OF EXPECTATIONS

Are there those in Judaism who believe the prophecy?

RABBI CITES PROPHECY: WAR HERALDS MESSIAH
DATELINE: SAN FRANCISCO, FEBRUARY 1, 1991

The Persian Gulf war will end by Purim and the Messiah will come soon thereafter.

Those predictions, made last week by a Lubavitcher rabbi, update a forecast by Jewish scholars 1,800 years ago of the present-day war between Iraq and the U.S.-Allied Forces . . .

Ancient scholars predicted that the king of Persia (in this case Saddam Hussein, who has become that "king" because he has lorded over the Persian Gulf, according to [Rabbi Manis] Friedman) would go to war with an Arab king—in this case, Saudi Arabia's King Fahd.

. . . The scholars further divined that the Arab king would enlist the help of a world superpower—the United States, of course—and then global combat would ensue.

If the comparison is followed to the letter, the war soon will devastate the world and, in the process . . . rid the world of its evil ideologies.

At the conclusion of the great war, "all the nations of the world will panic, and tremble, and be thrown into confusion," explained Friedman. "Israel will panic and

[Jews] will say, 'Where should we go, where should we go?' "

But Jews there need not worry because God will spare Jerusalem from destruction, the way he is protecting Tel Aviv from Scud missiles . . .

Jews in Israel and the Diaspora need not worry the Gulf War will bring death and destruction to the Jewish state, he said.

"God says to us, do not be afraid, you have nothing to be afraid of. The time of your redemption has come . . . "

Each time the world has faced a catastrophe, Jews have said it was the time the Moshiach—Hebrew for Messiah—would come . . .

According to the rabbi, the coming of the Messiah already is behind schedule. "He has disappointed us enough times already. This time he has to come."

Of course, if he doesn't come, "we'll be angrier at him," said Friedman. "And when he finally does come, he'll need to do a lot of explaining."[5]

Rabbi Friedman might well have had his tongue somewhere in the vicinity of his cheek when he made that last comment. Sadly, even many who are "religious" miss the real point of prophecy. It was not primarily for us to know what we may expect of God. Its fundamental purpose is to communicate what God expects of us.

But whatever the good rabbi's intentions, it is evident that he shares a concern held by many who look on current events from the higher plane of awareness: Something big is in the wind!

Is it possible that the issue which will precipitate the next round of region-shaking strife and bring history one step closer to its fulfillment of the prophecy might be the Palestinian "problem"?

If some voices are heard . . .

Israel must now declare itself willing to abide by Security Council resolutions 242 and 338.[6]

Iraq's withdrawal will have impact in the Arab world, and I expect that will bring international attention to a peaceful solution for the Palestinian question, which after all is the mother of all instability in the Middle East.[7]

Is it possible that Messiah is going to return as Lovelle Williams and the rabbis believe?

Will the removal of one Saddam
create 100 others?

---

10. THE MIDDLE EAST TODAY — HOW DID WE GET TO WHERE WE ARE?

ARAB MUSLIMS AND SADDAM HUSSEIN — ISHMAEL THE CHOSEN?

It's clear from our discussion in the last chapter that the Jewish people have a deep sense of chosenness. What you may not be aware of is that the Arabs also feel a sense of chosenness — different from that of the Jews, but a similar sense nonetheless.

The roots of that feeling trace all the way back to Hebrew Scriptures. According to these accounts in the Bible, the son of the Covenant with the Jewish people —

118

Isaac—and the son of the Covenant with the Arab people—
Ishmael—were brothers of the same father—Abraham.

Both peoples arise from a common Chaldean ancestry,
born in antiquity in strife and anguish, continuing to this
day in strife and anguish.

Who are the descendants of Ishmael?

H. A. R. Gibb, the eminent British historian of the
Arab peoples, presented this now famous definition: "All
those are Arabs for whom the central fact of history is the
mission of Muhammad and the memory of the Arab Empire
and who in addition cherish the Arabic tongue and its
cultural heritage as their common possession."[1]

Of course this is not a complete definition. That is
impossible. The Arab people are far too diverse. Today
there are Arab Christians and Arabs who adhere to other
religions. In the past, there were Arabs before Muhammad.

In antiquity, the descendants of Ishmael were desert
tribesmen, skilled warriors and ferocious fighters. Some
migrated east and settled in the broad, fertile valleys of the
Tigris and Euphrates rivers. There they contributed to the
dynasties that became the superpowers of the Fertile Crescent.

Though Babylonia and Assyria both have long his-
tories that antedate Abraham, in later times the descendants of Ishmael made their own influential contributions
to these Mesopotamian powers. The Assyrians were the
most ruthless while the Babylonians were the most famous.
Both were located in territory which comprises modern
Iraq. This heritage has not been forgotten by the Arab
people living in that region today and has had a certain
effect on the dreams of grandeur nourished by Saddam
Hussein.

Other branches of the Ishmaelite family tree held to their nomadic traditions, wandering in and out of the deserts and the Fertile Crescent. As early as the first millennium B.C.E., when the great superpowers were thriving, these tribesmen already were being referred to as Arabs. Their neighbors to the north applied the term to a group of tribes in the northern part of the Arabian peninsula (modern Saudi Arabia). In the ancient language Akkadian, they were known as Aribi, Arabi, Arubu, and Urbu, and in Hebrew, as Arab.

The earliest appearance of the designation came in a regnal text of Shalmaneser III, the Assyrian. In 853 B.C.E, he defeated a coalition of Syrian and Israelite kings in Qarqar in Syria. Also in the coalition were 1000 cameleers "from Gindibu in the Arabi country."

The decline of the great superpowers, Assyria and Babylon, after the middle of the last millennium before the common era, led to decay in the area. The once fabulously wealthy empires were reduced again to tribal confederations and fiercely independent warring factions.

It does appear that there were sporadic attempts at unification of the disparate tribes even though none were ultimately successful. The earliest inscription in true Arabic is on the tombstone of a king named Imru'ul-Qays who died in 328 B.C.E. Located on the edge of the Syrian desert near Namara, this tombstone declares Imru'ul-Qays "king of all the Arabs." We have no historical record to corroborate his claim, but apparently he had at least tried to unite the tribes, although to no lasting avail.

This state of affairs persisted for centuries. While the Chinese flourished with a spectacular culture far to the east and the Greeks and Romans flourished in the west, the Arab tribesmen remained primitive and fierce.

As the centuries passed, a common culture slowly emerged from common practices and growing interaction. The tribes were animists and shared many religious shrines. They also participated in great fairs during which there were literary and oratorical contests between tribes. They made sacred truces, shared a common calendar, and fought mutual enemies.

These people were slowly heading toward a singular identity. They were ripe for a leader to unite them.

Then Muhammad came.

THE COMING OF THE PROPHET

In a cave at the foot of Mount Hira near Mecca, where he had spent six months in solitary meditation, Muhammad received a vision. The angel Gabriel roused him from his bed with the stern command: "Proclaim!"

Rubbing his eyes, the startled Muhammad gasped, "But what shall I proclaim?"

"Proclaim in the name of the Lord, the Creator who created man from a clot of blood! Proclaim! Your Lord is most gracious. It is he who has taught man by the pen that which he does not know."

Thus it was, according to Islamic tradition, that an unremarkable Arab trader from Mecca was inspired to preach God's word in the year A.D. 610.[2]

Muhammad captured the Arab imagination. He and his growing body of converts increasingly appealed to the emerging Arab cultural identity. He sought to turn them from their many paths, their many gods and their independent ways, and to rally them to Allah and a single path.

He enjoyed spectacular success, both during and after his own lifetime: Less than a hundred years after the death of Muhammad in A.D. 632, his followers had burst out of the Arabian desert to conquer and create an empire whose glories were to shine for a thousand years. . . . they conquered the Persian Empire and much of the Byzantine, spreading the faith through the Middle East to the Indus River. From there, devout Arab traders later carried their faith to Malaysia, Indonesia, Singapore and the Philippines. Other traders introduced the Koran to black tribes of Africa that lived south of the Sahara Desert.[3]

The reason for this incredible spread of the religion of the Prophet lay in a primal religious motivation: If Islam was the truth as revealed by God, it would be scandalous if its adherents neglected telling anyone of it.

Two things you have to keep in mind about this early period of Islam which will help you better understand its 20th century form. First, the terms "Arab" and "Muslim" are not synonymous. In those early centuries, all Arabs were required to become Muslim, i.e., to practice Islam. Many other peoples, from Asia to Africa, also became Muslim, but that did not make them Arab.

"Arab" refers to ethnic identity, "Muslim" to religious practice. Today there are Arabs who are not Muslim, and Arabs who confess Jesus as Lord or who practice other religions, but they are definitely in the minority.

The second thing to keep in mind is this: Following the death of Muhammad, coinciding with the tremendous expansion, a fundamental division occurred in the ranks of the Arab Muslims. The Prophet's male children all died in childhood, leaving no heir apparent. To exacerbate the problem, he left no generally accepted instructions on how the leadership of the movement should be handled after his death.

Two factions developed. One held that the leader should be nominated by representatives of the community and confirmed by an oath of allegiance made by the representative. Those who held these views called themselves "Sunni" (from *sunna,* "the tradition of the Prophet"). The other group insisted that Muhammad's spiritual authority was passed on to his cousin and son-in-law, 'Ali, and to certain of his direct descendants known as Imams. This group became known as Shi'ites or Shi'a Muslims, "partisans of 'Ali."

Today, 90 percent of all Muslims are Sunni, including the Saudis, the Kuwaitis, and the Ba'ath party of Iraq headed (at this writing) by Saddam Hussein.

But in modern Iran and Iraq, part of the heartland of Islam, the overwhelming majority of the Arab populations are Shi'ite.

INTO THE MODERN WORLD

Later, Islam fought successfully to preserve its ideological integrity in the face of Mongol invaders, Western Crusaders, and more recently, Western imperialists. But by the end of World War I, the Ottoman Empire had been dismembered and large portions of it brought under the domination of the colonizing nations of Christian Europe.[4]

Phenomenal growth marked the golden age of Islam. But by the days of the rise of modern Western imperialism, Islam's incredible military, political and cultural power was on the wane, leaving the Islamic lands vulnerable to encroachment by Westerners. In fact, in many of those Islamic lands, the Muslim natives had become subjugated peoples who struggled for independence.

Living under colonial rule set another fire burning in the hearts of modern Arabs and Muslims: Islam must exercise temporal as well as spiritual power. Muslims, who believed that Allah himself is to rule Islamic society through the holy men, could not accept exterior rule imposed by polytheist Westerners (the Muslim view of the Christian Trinity is that the belief affirms three "gods").

So as the decades of the 20th century filled the hourglass, the fervor of Islam as a political as well as theological driving force filled the hearts of Muslims, especially the Arabs under British occupation.[5]

At the same time that Zionists were working toward a Jewish homeland in the region of Palestine, Arab nationalists were struggling for their own self-determination.

Also, the British were feeling pressures from home to get out of Mesopotamia.

The time was right for historic changes.

In March of 1921, four years after the Balfour Declaration and the British Mandate for Palestine, the British called a conference of leaders of their Arab colonies at Cairo. Colonial Secretary Winston Churchill carved out four-fifths of what was then called Palestine and created the country of Trans-Jordan (now known as the Hashemite Kingdom of Jordan under King Hussein). The remaining one-fifth was the territory pledged by the Balfour Declaration to be governed in favor of the Zionists.

That left a terrible, smoldering problem: What about the Arabs of Palestine (both Muslim and Christian Palestinians) who remained in the territory dedicated by the British to Zionist benefit?

They were descendants of Bedouin tribesmen who had finally settled in the hills of Palestine, in a sense as squatters in Ottoman Turk territory. After all these years, they felt this land was their home, if not their nation.

At that same conference, decisions were made regarding the territories in the Persian Gulf. The modern boundaries of the countries in the region were set, again rather arbitrarily, and again, in a way that left territorial disputes the smoldering issue in the region.

THE POT BOILS OVER

The territorial dispute (coupled with political and economic ambitions) that has most affected us in the early months of the 1990s has its roots in that same conference.

Secretary Churchill combined three provinces in Mesopotamia — Mosul, Baghdad and Basra — to form modern Iraq. It was made a kingdom under British Mandate with Faisal I as its regent. After just over a decade, the kingdom shed its colonial connections and became an independent political entity in 1932.

The internal developments that followed were complicated and tragic. For three decades, the anti-Western sentiments, the pan-Arab nationalism, and the old loyalties to family, tribe and religion combined in an explosive and bloody series of coups and counter-coups. The monarchy ultimately fell, and in 1968 a socialist Ba'ath regime gained power.

In that year the Revolutionary Command Council was formed by leaders of the various anti-monarchy parties. The Council assumed supreme authority over the government, and immediately, the Ba'ath faction engaged in a power struggle with the Iraqi Prime Minister, Nayif-Daud and his party.

On July 30, 1968, a group of officers under the command of Saddam Hussein arrested Nayif and installed a regime so ruthless that all opposition was simply crushed.

Saddam Hussein became the key to Iraq's national stability.

He was placed in charge of internal security.

To provide that stability, he resorted to brutal repression. He formed a terrifying intelligence network which he then used to gain personal power. Over the years he murdered both his enemies and his friends until he finally reached the top rung of the ladder.

Though President Bakr continued to preside over the Revolutionary Command Council and the Iraqi Regional Council (during the '70s), Saddam Husayn, leader of the coup of July 30, 1968, emerged as the unrivalled leader not only in Ba'th circles but also in the country as a whole. In July 1979 Bakr resigned and Husayn succeeded as president of the republic in accordance with the temporary constitution. He promptly suppressed the Iraqi Communist Party and all other opponents.[6]

ARAB AND JEW — BLOOD BROTHERS OR BLOOD ENEMIES?

The Arabs are a noble people with a history that stretches back into time immemorial. They are not and have never been sneaky, crafty sheep stealers, a "filthy race," as some have unfairly labeled them. They are descendants of a highly disciplined, organized and durable people from a desert environment where life was hard and survival pre-eminent.

During the Dark Ages in Europe the great advances in knowledge made by the Greeks and the Romans were in danger of being tragically lost. It was the Muslims in Africa and the Middle East who preserved the great heritage of the Western World.

And during that long period of time, Arabs and Jews generally enjoyed good relations. Much medieval Jewish learning drew from and transmitted Arabic culture. In later centuries the Jewish and Arab peoples coexisted peacefully in Palestine—before the British Mandates.

The serious problems began in the days following World War I when the British arbitrarily assigned borders in this former Imperial territory. Suddenly, peaceful coexistence became impossible because national identity was at stake.

Besides the borders being drawn on maps, there were lines drawn in the sand. The Dome of the Rock, a fairly unimportant shrine for centuries, was elevated to the position of second holiest shrine in Islam, largely, some think, as a defense against what some people viewed as the "encroachment of Zionism."

The Palestinians were understandably gripped with a feeling of helplessness over the shifting future and status of the land they had always considered their home. After 1948, when many ended up in refugee camps in the West Bank and Gaza, that feeling of helplessness grew to despair, anger and finally, revolution.

Zionists, in turn, have understandably held to an unshakable commitment that—especially in light of the Holocaust—the Jewish people not only deserve a homeland but cannot survive without one.

When, in 1967, Egypt announced a blockade on the Gulf of Aqaba—cutting off the Israeli port of Eilat and violating international agreements—President Nasser was in fact committing an act of aggression that inevitably led to war. In response to this action, President Lyndon Johnson pronounced:

> If a single act of folly was more responsible for this explosion than any other it was the arbitrary and dangerous announced decision that the Strait of Tiran would be closed. The right of innocent maritime passage must be preserved for all nations.[7]

Meanwhile, the Soviets not only were continuing their support of Nasser, but they also began supplying Syria with new military and economic aid. During the first four months of 1967, there were thirty-seven raids made on Israel as well as Syrian shelling of Israeli villages from the Golan Heights.

When, in April, the Syrians attacked Israeli tractors with machine guns, tanks and heavy mortars, Israeli planes took off and took out six Syrian Migs.

On May 18, the Voice of the Arabs announced:

> As of today, there no longer exists an international emergency force to protect Israel. We shall exercise patience no more. We shall not complain any more to the U.N. about Israel. The sole method we shall apply against Israel is a total war which will result in the extermination of Zionist existence.[8]

On May 20, Hafez Assad, then Syria's Defense Minister, added to the threat of war:

> Our forces are now entirely ready not only to repulse the aggression, but to initiate the act of liberation itself, and to explode the Zionist presence in the Arab homeland.[9]

On May 28, 1967, Egyptian President Nasser left no question as to his intent to destroy Israel when he stated, "We will not accept any . . . coexistence with Israel. . . . Today the issue is not the establishment of peace between the Arab states and Israel. . . . The war with Israel is in effect since 1948."[10]

On May 30, Jordan's King Hussein went to Cairo and signed a five-year mutual defense pact with Egypt; Israel now had a hostile Arab alliance on three frontiers.

Iraq also joined the alliance, and on May 31, Iraqi President Aref declared: "The existence of Israel is an error which must be rectified. This is our opportunity to wipe out the ignominy which has been with us since 1948. Our goal is clear—to wipe Israel off the map."[11] These developments among Arab leaders are often overlooked when people speak of the 1967 war. In response to the threats that had been made and to prevent their being wiped off the map, the Israelis struck on June 5, 1967 in what would become known as the Six-Day War. Once Israel took East Jerusalem and unified the city, there was never a thought of ever giving it up again.

The divisions widened and positions hardened.

MORE OF THE SAME IN THE DECADE OF THE '90s?

Have the tensions decreased since the '67 war? Hardly. Another war was fought in 1973 with another brilliant victory for the Israelis. In 1982, Israelis bombed an Iraqi nuclear reactor to deprive Saddam Hussein of an ultimate threat to Israeli security. And during the 1980s, violent upheavals among Palestinians in the occupied territories galvanized into an organized rebellion—the intifada.

Both sides have become firmly entrenched. Israeli leader Ariel Sharon has stated:

> We have one interest. We want to live here peacefully and defend our lives. We will pay no price to anyone. . . . Jerusalem is not negotiable. It will never be negotiable. Jerusalem is the heart of the Jews. It has been the capital of the Jews for the last 3,000 years. We will accept no other arrangement.[12]

On the other side, consider Saddam Hussein's motives in the Arab-Israeli tensions:

> What is most important to me about Nebuchadnezzar [the ancient king of Babylon] is the link between the Arabs' abilities and the liberation of Palestine. Nebuchadnezzar was, after all, an Arab from Iraq, albeit ancient Iraq. Nebuchadnezzar was the one who brought

the bound Jewish slaves from Palestine. That is why, whenever I remember Nebuchadnezzar, I like to remind the Arabs — Iraqis in particular — of their historical responsibilities. It is a burden that should not stop them from action, but rather spur them into action because of their history.[13]

Is it any wonder that among Palestinians and other radical Arabs there grew up a personality cult around Saddam Hussein, the one they believed to be the deliverer of the Palestinian people and a modern-day Saladin? From *USA Today*, in the weeks between the beginning of the bombing of Iraq by the Allies and the end of the Persian Gulf War:

> Saddam's cult-like following is high in the Middle East. And nowhere is that more apparent than in Jordan and the occupied territories in nearby Israel. Saddam's photo hangs in most schools, businesses, homes and taxis here, even bathrooms. His face is on buttons and watches; children have changed the traditional Moslem greeting of Salaamu Alaikum, "Peace be unto you," to Saddam Alaikum, "Peace be unto Saddam." At least 412 newborns have been named after Saddam, who was almost unheard of in the West before Iraq's August 2 invasion of Kuwait . . .

> Despite heavy war losses, Saddam's popularity rests on his promise to fight for the Palestinian cause and in "standing up to" the West. For Palestinians, who make up 60 percent of Jordan's 3.4 million people, he is their savior.[14]

"But Saddam Hussein is history," one might object, and rightfully so. However, the issue before us, especially in light of biblical prophecy, is not Saddam Hussein. The issue is what Saddam Hussein represented. This has never been expressed better than by Egyptian columnist Mohamed Sayed Ahmed:

Saddam's standing up to [George] Bush is the catalyst for the acceleration of history in the Middle East. We know he will not win the war. What we do not know is whether the removal of one Saddam will create 100 others.[15]

I JUST DON'T UNDERSTAND!

For North Americans, the events surrounding the Persian Gulf War and the Arab-Israeli conflict are sometimes hard to understand. Why would Saddam Hussein cause his own people to be bombed almost out of existence and still consider the Iraqi effort a victory? How could he possibly present himself as the one who will save and deliver his brothers, the Palestinians, by conquering all opposition, including the U.N. Coalition Forces, and especially the Jewish people?

Grasping the reality of a completely other way of thinking is crucial if we are to see how a prophecy which seems like fantasy to a snug, comfortable North American could be fulfilled in our world. "This is the Middle East," says Kamel Abu Jaber, a Jordanian political scientist. "Always there is an interchange between myth and reality."[16]

In the Middle East, a sense of reality doesn't come from current events. It comes from what the religion of the realm says reality is.

THE RISE OF THE SPIRIT OF ANTICHRIST

The Bible refers to this attitude, which combines self-appointment to the office of "savior" with hatred of the Jewish people, as the spirit of Antichrist.

The authentic Christ, Jesus of Nazareth, came to earth as Savior. His divine task was to deliver human beings from the oppression of sin and its results in the world.

In the Bible, Antichrist is not a person or a force seeking to do battle with Christ. He appears as a "Christ" or messiah who appoints himself as savior in place of Jesus of Nazareth.

He is the one who, in the last days, the masses will believe to be their savior.

The Antichrist is an ominous counterfeit savior. He hates the Jewish people because he hates the God of the Bible. The Antichrist has a three-pronged vision for the world under his leadership. That vision includes politics, economics and religion. He is self-exalting to the point of demanding veneration from his followers.

HUSSEIN THE ANTICHRIST?

The rabbi Saul (Paul) of Tarsus wrote:

> Concerning the coming of our Lord Jesus Christ and our being gathered to him, we ask you, brothers, not to become easily unsettled or alarmed by some prophecy, report or letter supposed to have come from us, saying that the day of the Lord has already come. Don't let anyone deceive you in any way, for that day will not come until the rebellion occurs and the man of lawlessness is revealed, the man doomed to destruction. He will oppose and will exalt himself over everything that is called God or is worshiped (2 Thessalonians 2:1-4).

Can you see the parallels between this "man of lawlessness" and Saddam Hussein? Exalting self, a rebellious spirit, one doomed to destruction. That self-exaltation fueled and was fueled by the worship-like attitude many Arabs held (and some still hold) toward the man. What is utterly inconceivable to us in the West became commonplace with Saddam in his heyday. One last point regarding biblical prophecy:

> From a biblical point of view, as we contemplate the tribulation period [a term for the period immediately

preceding the coming of Christ], Babylon becomes prominent in the prophetic future. John devoted two chapters in the book of Revelation to Babylon, and this was intended to signify the importance of this area in the end times just prior to the kingdom of peace.[17]

Is Saddam Hussein, ruler of modern Babylon, the Antichrist? I hardly think so. But as much as any other man who ever lived, he has represented the spirit of Antichrist about which the Bible warns.

Roger Stanley may have been right when, in the Merit High School teachers' lounge, he laid the problems we're facing in the Middle East at the feet of the British and their post-Imperial policies. But Lovelle Williams might just also be right, not about what caused the problems, but about where they're leading us. The defiant spirit of Saddam Hussein, the adoration of him by masses of Arabs, the weddedness of Israel to Jerusalem—all may be signs of more biblical prophecy being fulfilled before our eyes, the beginning of the end, the overture to Armageddon.

What if the Gulf War
had happened this way?

11. A NEW WORLD ORDER

**This is not that, but it is like that,
and it is leading up to that!
—John Latimer**

Right up front let me say that I do not now, nor have I ever, believed that Saddam Hussein is the Antichrist, the man of lawlessness. Nor did I believe that the recent crisis in the Persian Gulf would bring Messiah's return.

However, I do believe that the forces at work in the recent crisis, when coupled with other phenomena of modern world politics, present us with an overture to Armageddon. The circumstances are right for a similar crisis to develop into the cataclysmic events that will bring Jesus the Messiah back to earth.

To demonstrate how extremely plausible this kind of development is, consider the following scenario:

It is early January, 1991. President Bush has not yet ordered Desert Storm. The Congress has not yet debated the issue of military engagement of Iraq. The massive bombing of Iraq and Kuwait has not yet begun.

Change just one element, one single element of the situation, and the euphoria over the success of Desert Storm might have been, instead, a whole set of emotions of another kind:

DATELINE: WASHINGTON, D.C.
SUNDAY, JANUARY 6, 1991

At 12:17 A.M. Sunday morning, President George Walker Bush suffered a massive stroke and is now in a deep coma at Walter Reed Army Medical Center. After an emergency meeting of the President's Cabinet in conjuction with House and Senate leaders, Chief Justice William Rehnquist administered the oath of office of President of the United States to Dan Quayle.

President Quayle issued a brief statement following the 4:30 A.M. ceremony in which he pledged to continue the policies of Mr. Bush, especially vis-a-vis Operation Desert Shield. "Preserving the remarkable international coalition forged by George Bush to liberate Kuwait is my top priority. His vision was one of a New World Order. I hereby commit myself to see that vision become a reality, beginning with the successful prosecution of our policy in the Persian Gulf."

Meanwhile, in another part of the world, another council was being held by others significantly affected by President Bush's stroke. Saddam Hussein called his own private conference at 1:00 P.M. Baghdad time, only minutes after the news of the transition of power was announced over CNN. In a closed session of the Revolutionary Council, Hussein ordered two immediate military actions to be taken. First, he instructed his senior Army commander to mobilize half of his occupation force in Kuwait. He was to seize the opportunity and make a lightning incursion into the oil fields of northwest Saudi Arabia, thereby flanking coalition forces gathering along the Kuwaiti border and the Gulf Coast. "You are to occupy the oil fields or you are to destroy them!"

Second, he ordered the immediate beginning of Scud missile attacks against Israel and Saudi Arabia.

At the conclusion of the meeting of the Revolutionary Council, Hussein boarded his private jet and made a clandestine flight into Tehran, Iran, for a secret meeting with Iranian President Rafsanjanii. In that meeting, the two old enemies agreed to unite against the "American Satan" in their turmoil following the welcome demise of Bush. "It is God's will!" they pledged. "He has granted this boon."

According to the agreement, Iraq would destroy or cripple the massive Saudi oil production facilities to further slow delivery of crude to the West. Iran would fortify her borders along the eastern shore of the Gulf with missiles and then stop all tanker traffic in and out of the Gulf at the Straits of Hormuz.

The two agreed further that if the forces of the gathering international coalition were to move on Iraq or Kuwait, Iran would join the battle and force the alliance to fight on an additional front.

*   *   *

While shockwaves reverberated through the media following the President's stroke, three significant events occurred, two highly visible, one invisible.

By the close of trading on Monday the 7th, prices on the New York Stock Exchange plummeted in an all-time record drop. The market fought off almost apoplectic investor fears that Quayle would not be able to navigate the treacherous international waters stirred by Iraq's August 2nd invasion of Kuwait. At the same time, oil prices soared while gold and commodities traders reported their worst day in history.

In the week immediately following Bush's demise, the Congress took up debate on the continued employment of sanctions against Iraq as an offensive strategy versus the use of military force. By Friday evening, both the House and Senate returned overwhelming votes: the administration must allow time for sanctions to work. Almost every congressman and senator argued that without Bush and his unique postion of leadership in the world community, military action would be sheer folly.

The third development, unknown to the general public, was that the U.S. State Department pledged to the Soviet Ambassador to honor the private Bush/Gorbachev "understanding" reached only hours before the President's stroke. The "understanding" was that a month after the successful resolution of the Gulf Crisis, the two nations would convene an International Peace Conference on the Middle East which would deal specifically with the Palestinian problem. It was a private agreement made by Bush to relieve Soviet pressure on the Baltic states. It was kept private to deprive Saddam Hussein of any propaganda advantage.

* * *

By the Friday of the Congressional vote, Israel had suffered light damage and only a few casualties from fourteen Scud missile attacks. U.S. Patriot missiles had been effective. Pressure on Israel to retaliate was intense, but coalition leaders succeeded in convincing Prime Minister Yitzhak Shamir to delay any retaliatory action.

The world press billed Shamir's restraint as a tremendous sacrifice. What they weren't picking up was that the restraint was entirely in his self-interest. His most daunting Arab foe was being threatened by a massive international force, his government was scoring valuable points in

Washington, and most Israeli citizens were against immediate retaliation.

Even so, he did plan to retaliate. Saturday night, following the Congressional vote and the Jewish Shabbat, he called a secret council of his Likud party leaders with the pivotal but fickle leaders of the Orthodox parties who had been the most vocal critics of Shamir's "no-retaliation" policy.

In the secret council, Prime Minister Shamir announced that he would be retaliating for those attacks, but that it would be Saddam Hussein who would bear the brunt of that retaliation, not the Iraqi people. He refused to give details but vowed that Israel would present secure borders and a safe homeland for the unprecedented wave of Jewish immigrants expected in the next months from the Soviet Union and Eastern Europe.

The meeting was closed with Shamir's pledge that the action would occur very soon.

*   *   *

Reaction to the Iraqi invasion of the Saudi oil fields was swift but painful. President Quayle issued orders to Supreme Commander Schwartzkophf: "Operation Desert Shield is a defensive deployment. You may repulse the Iraqi troops from the Saudi oil fields and you may destroy Scud launch sites in Iraq, but you must not engage in offensive maneuvers of any other kind. The Congress has ordered it, and the coalition is teetering on dissolution. We must stay the course set by my predecessor."

General Schwartzkophf did repel the invading force from the Saudi oil fields, but not before the Iraqis had implemented a scorched earth campaign against those oil fields. Hundreds of wellheads were ignited and storage facilities destroyed by explosives.

In the meantime, mobile Iranian Silkworm missiles were scoring deadly successes in the Gulf shipping lanes as they destroyed dozens of oil tankers heading for the Far East and for Western countries.

The flow of oil from the Persian Gulf was virtually shut off. World financial markets responded with day after day of record losses. Inflation in the West increased to double-digit levels almost overnight.

*   *   *

With the continuing Scud missile attacks against Tel Aviv, Hussein hoped to bait Israel into entering the fray and further weakening the coalition. Night after night, dozens of missiles flew over Israel while Patriot missiles continued performing brilliantly in protecting the Israeli citizenry.

On the seventh night of air raid sirens, a veritable tidal wave of missiles swept over the Judean hills. More than 100 Scuds were counted—by far the largest attack yet and far too many to be met effectively by the anti-missile systems. However, only eight of the missiles landed in Jewish neighborhoods, causing only minor damage. Two of the missiles landed on the Temple Mount in Jerusalem, demolishing the two Arab mosques on the site. The remaining swarm fell on Arab neighborhoods and refugee camps in the West Bank and Gaza. Hundreds of Palestinians were killed, including most of the key leaders of the territories and of the intifada.

The Muslim world erupted in anger against Saddam Hussein. Even the Palestinians living in Jordan, people who had lionized him before, turned on him with a vengeance. Trucks streamed across the Jordanian/Iraqi border, filled with irate Palestinians bound for Baghdad. These men were determined to find and kill Saddam Hussein, even if the only way to do that was to drown him in their blood as they fell upon his bunker, martyred by Iraqi bullets.

*   *   *

In truth, the fusillade of missiles had not all come from Iraq—only the ones which hit Jewish neighborhoods. The rest were Scud-class missiles launched by Israelis from mobile launchers deployed deep in the Judean wilderness, near the Israeli/Jordanian border.

Yitzhak Shamir had his revenge.

*   *   *

In the United States, President Quayle was reeling under the weight of the problems caused by the cutoff of Gulf oil and the continuing intransigence of the Iraqis. His approval rating was plummeting as rapidly as the stock market.

But worse, the oil drought brought on by the Iraq/Iran actions had precipitated hyperinflation in many developing countries, along with the most alarming inflation rate the West had seen in this century. As a result, in one four-day period, the governments of Mexico, Brazil, Venezuela, Irian Jaya, Bolivia and Zimbabwe all defaulted on their development loans from U.S. and other international banks.

That blow was too much for the already-weakened U.S. banking system. Four of the five largest banks collapsed during that week, followed by the closing of hundreds of smaller banks nationwide.

The Federal Reserve tried to cope with the problem but simply was overwhelmed. In response, they ordered all banks and S&Ls to close their doors until further notice. Trading at the NYSE and Chicago Board of Trade also was suspended indefinitely.

The Congress was in disarray. President Quayle authorized limited offensive maneuvering by coalition troops in the Gulf, but only those actions intended to free the flow of oil and relieve the inflationary pressures.

*   *   *

Saddam Hussein at first was alarmed by news of the bloody missile barrage on Arabs in the Green Line Territories and the Holy Places, Sharam es Sharif and the El Aksa Mosque. But instinctively, he knew what had happened. He even appreciated the brilliant move by the Israelis.

And in it, he saw opportunity.

He decided that with the West in financial chaos and their will to fight in the Persian Gulf eroding hourly, there was a greater prize than Kuwait.

First, he ordered high-level meetings between his top aides and the leaders of every Muslim nation on earth, including the Arab members of the International Coalition, except the Saudis and the Kuwaitis. In the meetings, the aides were to explain the Israeli ruse and what Hussein intended to do about it, and they were to implore their Muslim brothers to unify under his leadership to deal with the Zionist problem once and for all.

Virtually all agreed.

Second, the wave of Palestinians rushing toward Baghdad was met by Republican Guard tanks along with Hussein himself. His personal appearance mollified them, and his stirring speech relit their anger. He explained the ruse, asked for their continued support, and cheered them as they turned back to Jordan and the renewal of the intifada—this time with a vengeance.

*   *   *

In the West, the International Coalition was straining to the breaking point. The Saudis and Kuwaitis continued to press for decisive action, but the Egyptians and Syrians did an about-face. They were pulling out. Saddam's emissaries had reached them. The U.S., the Europeans and the Turks all felt massive pressure to disengage. The economic chaos was exacting a terrible toll.

*   *   *

That's when Saddam Hussein called the news conference.

He announced that he was a man of peace who, more than Western leaders, wanted to see a New World Order based on justice. Because of that, he would withdraw immediately and unilaterally from Kuwait as a show of good faith. In addition, he agreed to honor all of the Security Council resolutions, including the payment of reparations to Kuwait. And he promised an expeditious resumption of oil flow from the Gulf.

Finally, as a gesture of good will and as a pledge of his desire for the New World Order, he would fund the construction of a House of Prayer for All Nations on Temple Mount in Jerusalem, to replace the Muslim mosques his own missiles had so tragically destroyed. It would be a holy site for all faiths, not just for the Muslims.

He didn't mention the Palestinians. And they didn't protest.

*   *   *

The coalition was euphoric! World financial markets rallied as oil prices dropped dramatically. It seemed that an end to the turmoil was in sight.

*　　*　　*

As the months passed, economic conditions failed to improve significantly. It seemed that the forces which had nudged the West into a recession at about the time of Saddam's invasion of Kuwait were now forces propelling depression, exacerbated by the collapse of the banking industry.

*　　*　　*

Still, Saddam Hussein kept his word. Within fourteen days, every Iraqi soldier was out of Kuwaiti territory and he was paying reparations to the government of the Emir.

*　　*　　*

And then, seven months after the end of the crisis, it happened. During the final days of the Gulf crisis, after executing his plan for retaliation against Hussein by secretly launching the missiles into the West Bank, Yitzhak Shamir appointed extremist ex-General Rehavam Ze'evi as Minister Without Portfolio and member of the Cabinet's Defense Committee. The appointment had shocked even Shamir's supporters because Ze'evi and his Moledet Party advocated a Transfer Policy—the transfer of the 1.7 million Palestinians living in the Green Line Territories (the West Bank and Gaza) to neighboring Arab states. In spite of the shock, Shamir won Ze'evi's appointment. It was clear to all that he was shoring up the Israeli government against any future political offensive by Washington.

Yitzhak Shamir had carefully planned and patiently bided his time for this moment. Seven months after the appointment, in response to the massive waves of Jewish immigrants from the Soviet Union and Eastern Europe, Ze'evi and Shamir won approval of the Transfer Policy. There simply must be more land made available.

In the early days of August, one year after Saddam Hussein first invaded Kuwait, the Israeli defense forces began mass deportation of Palestinians.

*   *   *

Saddam Hussein struck hard and fast. He had proven his goodwill by faithfully fulfilling the U.N. Resolutions and by masterfully manipulating the leadership of Arab East Jerusalem so that a start actually had been made on the House of Prayer for All Nations. With that success and the backing of the Soviet Union, he flew to New York to address in person the United Nations on the Palestinian issue.

He insisted that the coalition which had been formed to enforce the will of the U.N. against his action in a legitimate border dispute now turn their attention to the rape of the Palestinians. "If the same world community which engaged Iraq in a noble struggle now turns a deaf ear to the Palestinian people and a blind eye to their Israeli oppressors, it is a community of hypocrites!"

Within hours of Saddam's speech, Soviet Foreign Minister Bessmertnych was in Washington conferring with President Quayle. "Mr. President," he said through his interpreter, "you and your nation have vacillated on this issue long enough. You must now honor the agreement made months ago by Mr. Bush and Premier Gorbachev. We must together convene a Peace Conference and bring this terrible injustice to a final resolution."

President Quayle acquiesced.

The United Nations gathered its delegates and appointed a special Commission on the Palestinian People, headed jointly by the U.S. and the U.S.S.R.

* * *

The Israeli government already had suspended the Transfer Policy in hopes of winning a better position. One week before the Commission report was due, they swallowed one more bitter pill in the interest of politics and allowed Saddam Hussein to attend the opening ceremonies for the House of Prayer for All Nations. Privately, Hussein arranged with the Arab leaders of East Jerusalem for the erection of a statue of himself to be set in the inner reaches of the facility, reasoning that he was due the honor by virtue of his great sacrifice on behalf of this project and world peace.

When the first of the Jewish Temple Mount extremists touring the building came upon the statue, they exploded in anger and precipitated a monumental riot among the already-hostile Jewish crowds. This statue on this site was, as far as they were concerned, the abomination of desolation spoken of by Daniel the prophet.

During the riot, Saddam Hussein was shot in the head, hundreds of Arabs and Christians were trampled or beaten to death, and the Temple Mount Faithful stormed the facility and occupied it.

In the wake of the tragedy, Minister Ze'evi ordered the immediate resumption of the Transfer Policy. The Temple Mount Faithful, in tandem with the Orthodox, tore out all semblance of Muslim and Christian trappings from the House of Prayer and transformed it into a temple, *the* Temple—the Jewish Temple.

* * *

World reaction to the massacre and to Ze'evi's move also was immediate. The Commission on the Palestinian People recommended seven resolutions to the Security

Council, all of which were adopted. Among the resolutions were mandates for the following:

1. Israel must withdraw all troops and Israeli civilians from the West Bank, Gaza and East Jerusalem immediately, pulling back to within Israeli borders as they were before the 1967 war.

2. The West Bank shall from henceforth be governed under U.N. mandate and shall be known as Palestine, the official homeland of the Palestinian people.

3. Because of its central importance, East Jerusalem, including Temple Mount, is to become an international city under direct administration of the United Nations.

4. The coalition forces assembled to deal with the Persian Gulf crisis are hereby authorized to enforce these resolutions with any and all means necessary.

* * *

The Israelis were livid! In response to the Security Council vote, they stepped up Transfer activities and began to settle Soviet immigrants in the Green Line Territories as quickly as they deported Palestinians.

To the resolution regarding Jerusalem, they were especially defiant: "A Jew would die seven excruciating deaths before he would relinquish Jerusalem."

* * *

In spite of worsening economic conditions in the West, the coalition committed itself to resolving the Arab/Israeli conflict once and for all. Peace in the region could only help stabilize the world economy.

Three aircraft carrier groups entered the Mediterranean Sea from deployment in the Persian Gulf. Hundreds of planes landed at bases in Egypt, Sinai, Turkey, Cyprus, Greece, Syria and Lebanon. 250,000 coalition ground troops massed in Egypt, Syria and Lebanon. The 200,000 troops still on peacekeeping duty in Saudi Arabia were placed on alert and ordered to the Saudi/Jordanian border, less than 100 miles from Jerusalem.

* * *

The Jews prepared for the New Holocaust, the Time of Jacob's Trouble they had expected for millenia.

"This time," the rabbis insisted, "Messiah must come."

There will be no next time.

We can be certain that the prophecies
will be fulfilled, that Messiah will return.

12. THIS IS THAT, SO BE AWARE!

The fictional scenario you just read portrays one way the recent crisis could have been played out. I painted the picture in order to demonstrate that the events the Bible predicts are chillingly plausible for a world edging toward the 21st century. In light of that, let me direct your attention back to the question I raised earlier:

What has God revealed about the future?

The answer is crucial at this point, but let me caution you: While Scripture is clear in its prophetic predictions regarding the last days, we honestly can't be certain of the actual historical and sequential outworking of these predictions. They foresee forces at work in the world and events which will transpire, but many of the details will be distinctly discernible only after the events take place.

That's the way God meant it to be. The prophecies were not intended to tag a specific day or hour, but to make us aware of the era in which they would occur. The Bible even warns, very soberly, that "no one knows about that day or hour" (Matthew 24:36).

If you hear someone divining specifics about the return of the Messiah, turn around and walk away. They don't know what they are talking about.

Because we cannot be certain about all the specific outworkings, you should realize that the following material is my own view. Some of my fellow believers in Jesus agree with me while others who are at least as godly and astute have differing views.

There are many reasons students of the Bible disagree on specifics of yet-to-be-fulfilled prophecy, but we all agree on one central point: The signs of the times are whispering, "Jesus is coming. Jesus is coming."

There is an old story told by the rabbis about a dispute which arose after the Temple was rededicated by the Maccabees in 165 B.C.E. Antiochus Epiphanes—the Seleucid ruler who dominated Syria-Palestine from 175-164 B.C.E.—had desecrated the Temple by sacrificing a pig to Zeus on the holy altar.

After the Maccabean revolt restored self-rule to the Jewish people, the priests set about cleansing the altar, the furnishings, and the environs of the Temple. Every trace of the defiling blood and fat of the swine sacrifice had to be purged.

There was a stack of holy and consecrated stones set back out of the way in a portico of the Temple. They were the twelve stones the ancient Israelites had taken from the floor of the Jordan River as they crossed it miraculously under Joshua while entering the Promised Land (the story is found in chapter 4 of Joshua in the Jewish Scriptures). The stones were a memorial to that great event, a perpetual reminder of God's mighty acts on behalf of His people.

The problem was that these were porous stones. The Jewish priests knew of no way to be certain that all traces of any defiling pork blood had been obliterated from the consecrated stones.

The stones were holy, yet they might also be unholy.

One wise priest ordered the holy/unholy stones to be set aside in an area where they would cause no problem. "When Messiah comes, He will tell us what to do with them." That's how I feel about the signs of the times.

Many current events seem to be speaking to us of the Messiah's return, but we don't exactly know how to regard these events. They appear to be fulfillments of the prophecies, but there is always the possibility of tainting the interpreting of these events with our own opinions. How all the signs of the times fit together in God's scheme of things, no one can know for certain.

However, we can be certain that the prophecies will be fulfilled, that Messiah will return, and that when He does, all will be clear.

WHAT DOES GOD SAY ABOUT THE FUTURE?

Let me show you from Scripture three of the most important prophecies in which God reveals part of our future:

1. The regathering of Jewish people to the Promised Land.

2. A coalition of hostile nations gathering against Israel.

3. The rise of a man of lawlessness (Antichrist).

These are phenomena which will all unfold together. Look around you and watch for the development of these forces in the modern world.

THE JEWISH PEOPLE WILL RETURN
TO THE PROMISED LAND

Prophecy is quite specific in saying that in the last days—the days preceding Messiah's return—Jewish people will come from the Diaspora (the dispersion), also called the galut (the exile) and will resettle in Israel, the very land promised to Abraham and his descendants through Isaac. Read one of them:

> This is what the LORD Almighty says: "I will save my people from the countries of the east and the west. I will bring them back to live in Jerusalem; they will be my people, and I will be faithful and righteous to them as their God" (Zechariah 8:7).

Notice that the Lord said, "I will save my people from the countries of the east and the west." Regathering them from an ancient dispersion is one thing. Saving His people from the countries of the east and west is quite another.

One needs to consider only the course of modern Jewish history to be amazed at the accuracy of this prophecy. The horrible pogroms of Czarist Russia, the virulent anti-Semitism of the Western World, the Holocaust of this century in Europe, the constant threat of war by Arab peoples, and the repression in the Soviet Union and Eastern Europe—all are threats from which the Jewish people are being "saved" even as we are being "regathered" to the land of Israel.

Coincidence?

Consider these promises God made to Abraham's descendants:

> I will signal for them
>   and gather them in.
> Surely I will redeem them;
>   they will be as numerous as before.

Though I scatter them among the peoples,
   yet in distant lands they will remember me.
They and their children will survive,
   and they will return.
I will bring them back from Egypt
   and gather them from Assyria.
I will bring them to Gilead and Lebanon,
   and there will not be room enough for them.
They will pass through the sea of trouble
      (Zechariah 10:8-11).

In order for these prophecies to be fulfilled, the Jewish people had to have some sort of legal claim to the land. That claim came first in a pledge through the Balfour Declaration of 1917, and then by international recognition of Israeli statehood in May of 1948. Not until that time could those prophecies be fulfilled.

Now, they can be — and they are!

Notice several things in this prophecy. First, the regathering of the Jewish people will take place from the west (represented by Egypt) and from the east (represented by Assyria).

Second, there is a depiction of trouble from which our people must be "saved." And third, note the detail that "there will not be room enough for them."

Regarding the first two points, it is clear that the modern state of Israel is a fulfillment — whether it is the final fulfillment, we will know when Messiah comes.

The third point is a specific detail that goes beyond some of the poetic imagery. The prophet predicted that "there will not be room enough for them."

Land for settlement is already a pressing problem in Israel. The scenario in the preceding chapter, though fictionalized, was factual in many points — including the fact that there are some in Israel, albeit an extreme minority, who advocate the transport of the 1.7 million Palestinians from the occupied territories into neighboring Arab states.

This "Transfer Policy" is now championed by Rehavam Ze'evi in his newly created post of Minister Without Portfolio. His nomination was approved the week of February 18, 1991.

Supporters of this policy find its rationale in two areas: (1) by eliminating the presence of the Palestinians from the occupied territories, Israel would eliminate the intifada and its accompanying problems; and (2) the policy opens up large areas of land for the purposes of settlement.

With an expected avalanche of immigrants from the Soviet Union in 1991 and 1992 (some estimate as many as two million), the words of the prophecy take on fresh meaning. Once again, this is not a fictional scenario. These are events that you can watch on television or read about in your morning paper.

Compare them with Scripture.

Coincidence?

THE COALITION OF NATIONS AGAINST ISRAEL

There is a second element in this prophetic unfolding of events, a recurring theme in the overture to Armageddon. In the same era that the Jewish people return to the land, another sobering development will take place. An international coalition of military forces will move against Israel, specifically to capture Jerusalem.

As you read the selected prophecies included below, remember three things:

1. In order for "all nations" to send expeditionary forces against anyone, there has to be an institution which represents "all nations." Such an

institution never existed in human history before the League of Nations and later the United Nations. Before that, the prophecies could not have been fulfilled.

2. In order for "all nations" to send expeditionary forces against anyone, there had to be an act or an agency of that institution which could set a precedent for the body to take such drastic action. Such agency was exhibited for the first time in the crisis triggered by Saddam Hussein. Before that, the prophecies could not have been fulfilled.

3. Now they can be.

And now the prediction:

> This is the word of the LORD concerning Israel. The LORD, who stretches out the heavens, who lays the foundation of the earth, and who forms the spirit of man within him, declares: "I am going to make Jerusalem a cup that sends all the surrounding peoples reeling. Judah will be besieged as well as Jerusalem. On that day, when all the nations of the earth are gathered against her, I will make Jerusalem an immovable rock for all the nations. All who try to move it will injure themselves" (Zechariah 12:1-3).

There are three aspects of this prophecy which should jolt our attention. First, do you see how God identified Himself in the opening sentences? "The LORD, who stretches out the heavens,who lays the foundations of the earth, and who forms the spirit of man within him."

In this prophecy, God uses a rather lengthy name to identify Himself as the Creator. That was unusual, as God more often refers to Himself as "The LORD your God," or "The LORD Almighty," or even simply, "The LORD." The uniqueness of the lengthy appellation for "Creator" shows that what follows is of special and profound significance. Indeed, what follows does have ultimate and epic significance.

Given the ongoing importance of Israel and the Middle East in world affairs, I would say that an international military coalition moving against Jerusalem would qualify as significant, wouldn't you?

The second thing to notice is that this epic event will involve God's judgment upon the nations through the vehicle of Israel. The coalition will be built on hostility toward Jerusalem and the regathered Jewish people. By then Israel will be regarded as a problem intense enough to "send all the surrounding peoples reeling."

A "cup of reeling" is a symbol used in Scripture for God's judgment, as in this example from another ancient prophet:

> Therefore hear this, you afflicted one,
>   made drunk, but not with wine.
> This is what your Sovereign LORD says,
>   your God, who defends his people:
> "See, I have taken out of your hand
>   the cup that made you stagger;
> from that cup, the goblet of my wrath,
>   you will never drink again.
> I will put it into the hands of your tormentors,
>   who said to you,
>   'Fall prostrate that we may walk over you.'
> And you made your back like the ground,
>   like a street to be walked over" (Isaiah 51:21-23).

The third thing becomes clear when one looks at a map of either the ancient or the modern Middle East. Remember which nations will experience God's judgment? Those "surrounding" Israel.

Those nations were and still are composed of Arab peoples.

So, it is clear that the issue that will provoke the advance of international forces against Jerusalem is none other than Arab/Israeli tension, or even actual conflict in which Israel gains an exaggerated advantage which causes the nations to "reel."

Does that sound unlikely? What about the '67 and '73 Wars? Another event like either of those could indeed bring a united force against Israel.

There is another prophecy, even more grim, concerning the same attack on Israel:

> I will gather all the nations to Jerusalem to fight against it; the city will be captured, the houses ransacked, and the women raped. Half of the city will go into exile, but the rest of the people will not be taken from the city (Zechariah 14:2)

Notice that "all the nations" gather against Jerusalem in order to fight against it and the regathered Jews who possess it. Once again, an international coalition is being described.

Maybe you've noticed an apparent contradiction in the prophecies I've quoted. The prophecy from Zechariah 12:1-3 spoke of Jerusalem as an "immovable rock." In chapter 14, Zechariah speaks of the city being captured and pillaged. A contradiction?

Not at all. Zechariah 12 describes the effect of the siege on the coalition forces. Zechariah 14 describes the effect of the siege on Jerusalem and its inhabitants. The phrase "immovable rock" in Hebrew refers to the lower stone in a gristmill, the stone that remained stationary in the grinding process. Generally, it was a much larger stone than the millstone (the one that turned) and thus, very difficult to move.

So when he calls Jerusalem an "immovable stone," he didn't mean an unconquerable city. He meant that Jerusalem will be like the stationary stone in a mill—the enemy might not move it, but he's going to inflict a lot of pain.

In order for "all the nations" to send expeditionary forces against any one nation, there would have to be some political or military action which could trigger the international institution to take such drastic measures. What the world witnessed Saddam Hussein doing in the Gulf could well be a representation, a precursor, an overture, to such an event or situation.

THE MAN OF LAWLESSNESS

Zechariah was a Jewish prophet speaking in the sixth century B.C.E. The later authors of the New Testament, who were also Jewish writers, continued to address the issue of the last days.

One such writer was Saul of Tarsus, better known as the apostle Paul. Educated in Jerusalem at the feet of the famous rabbi Gamaliel, Paul was a Pharisee who had accepted Jesus as the Messiah. He was instrumental in bringing the message of the Messiah to the larger Gentile world. Part of that message was the prophetic understanding of events that were yet to unfold. Paul wrote many letters to individuals and gatherings of early believers with whom he had contact. Two of these were written to believers living in the Greek city of Thessalonica (Thess-ah-lon-I-ka). In each of the two letters, Paul gave what is explicitly a "more sure word of prophecy."

I want to focus on his second letter and his references to three significant forces which would be at work during the same period Zechariah described.

1. THE RISE OF THE MAN OF LAWLESSNESS

Paul wrote this to a congregation of believers in Jesus:

> Concerning the coming of our Lord Jesus Christ
> and our being gathered to him, we ask you, brothers, not
> to become easily unsettled or alarmed by some prophecy,
> report or letter supposed to have come from us, saying
> that the day of the Lord has already come. Don't let
> anyone deceive you in any way, for that day will not come
> until the rebellion occurs and the man of lawlessness is
> revealed, the man doomed to destruction. He will oppose
> and will exalt himself over everything that is called God
> or is worshiped, so that he sets himself up in God's
> temple, proclaiming himself to be God (2 Thessalonians
> 2:1-4).

You might remember that I referred to this passage
earlier in the book. I said that Saddam Hussein was not the
"man of lawlessness," known in other prophecies as the
Antichrist or the "Beast."

But it is apparent that Saddam exhibited what the
Bible terms the "spirit of Antichrist," in that he was one
doomed to destruction yet who exalts himself, behaving as
though he is above any law—as though he believed himself
to be some sort of a god.

Remember the oil slicks, the scorched earth?

Remember how Iraq was littered with Saddam
Hussein's own exalted, larger-than-life image?

Down through the centuries, many people have tried
to identify the "man of lawlessness" from imagery in the
passage quoted above, or from the book of Revelation. In
our time there have been "authorities" who dubbed Hitler,
John F. Kennedy, Henry Kissinger, and even Winston
Churchill as the Antichrist.

All were wrong!

The simple truth is that the spirit of Antichrist is now at work in the world and has been for a very long time. Exactly who the Antichrist will be is unknown, and guessing at the identity of the Antichrist is a waste of time. Even when the Antichrist rises to power there will be some doubt as to whether he is the one, because even he will have a seemingly good side. He will appear to work for peace in a clever ruse to advance his own agenda. Disorientation and deception will prevent the world from knowing with certainty his true identity until the cataclysm which he unleashes is upon the world.

That is why Paul wrote to the congregation at Thessalonica not to be distressed over mere rumors. When the time comes, there will be no doubt about it.

2. THE RESTRAINER

Paul continues his letter to the Thessalonians by saying:

> Don't you remember that when I was with you I used to tell you these things? And now you know what is holding him back, so that he may be revealed at the proper time. For the secret power of lawlessness is already at work; but the one who now holds it back will continue to do so till he is taken out of the way. And then the lawless one will be revealed, whom the Lord Jesus will overthrow with the breath of his mouth and destroy by the splendor of his coming (2 Thessalonians 2: 5-8).

Paul here explains why the man of lawlessness, the Antichrist, had not appeared in Paul's own day (the first century C.E.), and why to this day he has yet to appear: There is one who is holding him back.

The "restrainer" is God, particularly in His person as what the Bible calls the "Spirit of God" or the "Holy Spirit." The Spirit of God is mentioned in the very first verses of the Old Testament:

In the beginning God created the heavens and the earth. Now the earth was formless and empty, darkness was over the surface of the deep, and the Spirit of God was hovering over the waters (Genesis 1:1,2).

Ever since creation, He has been working in this world to bring order and to dispel the chaos that is associated with evil. Without God's Spirit at work in the world, the forces of evil would have run rampant.

Paul predicted that in the last days — the same period prophesied by Zechariah — the restrainer will remove His presence from the world. Chaos will emerge in the person of the man of lawlessness.

3. THE POWERFUL DELUSION

The coming of the lawless one will be in accordance with the work of Satan displayed in all kinds of counterfeit miracles, signs and wonders, and in every sort of evil that deceives those who are perishing. They perish because they refused to love the truth and so be saved. For this reason God sends them a powerful delusion so that they will believe the lie and so that all will be condemned who have not believed the truth but have delighted in wickedness (2 Thessalonians 2:9-12).

The third phenomenon which Paul said would take place in the last days is a "powerful delusion" which God would send those who willingly prefer falsehood to truth and evil to good. A delusion is anything which contradicts the truth God has communicated through His Messiah and through His self-revelation in the Scripture. It is the powerful force of an idea which holds the potential of truth, but not the substance.

Think about our earlier cast of characters: Sam, Evelyn, Tessie and Roger. All of them had searched for spiritual reality or had found something they believed to be true and real. But in searching, they willingly entered into the realm of the powerful delusion.

They looked in the realm of The Dark Saying hoping to find a source of light, not realizing that in the dimness of that region, nothing is really as it appears to be. They had not yet considered the one source on earth that claims for itself the distinction of being God's own revelation of Himself to human beings.

It is a powerful delusion indeed that causes otherwise rational people to search for light in some corner of the dark rather than searching for light in the light.

*"What will be the sign of Your coming
and of the end of the age?"*

13. AND ALL
THE NATIONS
WILL MOURN

As I am about to die, I want you to know . . .

Scripture secrets are not for the uninitiated. The Bible
has some hard sayings about the future. Humanly speaking, one needs to understand who is saying what in what
kind of situation. Generally speaking, we rightly presume
that when a person is coming to the end of life and is about
to go through the door of death he will utter the most
profound truths. The leaders of Judea couldn't have known
it, the Romans certainly didn't, nor could the citizens who
made up the mob—but a death sentence already had been
pronounced on Y'shua. It had been decided beyond eternity. The execution would take place in a week. He alone
knew it, and in view of what would happen, He remained
remarkably calm and even smiled as He approached the
Jerusalem He loved.

He came with His traveling seminary students. Some
of His disciples talked among themselves and openly
wondered if this was when He would announce His
kingship, claim the throne of David, and vanquish the

Romans. The Romans wondered if there would be trouble. They knew they needed to be on guard when the city was thronged with pilgrims.

The priests and Pharisees were watching to see if this clever man from Nazareth might finally trip Himself up so they could move on Him. The Pharisees were threatened by the fact that He did not accept the "rabbinical findings" as normative religion. Certainly some of the Sadducees knew He had said that if the Temple were destroyed, He would raise it up in three days. As guardians of the Temple established by God and rebuilt by Herod, this could only mean trouble.

One afternoon during that week, Jesus and His disciples left the Temple precincts where they had spent the day. They were heading for Bethany to spend the night there. As if they had never seen it before, and as if Jesus had not taught in its porticos, one of the disciples began acting as a guide. As though Jesus and the party were on their first pilgrimage to Jerusalem, this disciple spoke of the spectacular Temple facilities known throughout the ancient world for their grandeur. Then he shifted the subject to what he really purposed and bluntly asked if Jesus was ready to set up His kingdom at this time.

Jesus paused, then in a serious but quiet voice responded, "Do you see all these things? I tell you the truth, not one stone here will be left on another; every one will be thrown down."

This answer was most disappointing and not at all what they hoped He would say. His answer raised all kinds of questions, but they trudged on in silence.

After wending their way down the Temple Mount, they crossed over to the far side of the valley and continued up the path to the crest of the Mount of Olives. There they paused, rested, and gazed at the panoramic view of the city.

There, **the** disciples summoned their courage and asked Jesus: "When will this happen, and what will be the sign of Your coming and of the end of the age?"

To them it was a single question. They saw the destruction of Jerusalem and the climax of world history at the end of the age all in the same period of time. Jesus, perhaps because He knew that all those events would not occur simultaneously, treated them as three distinct questions, each requiring a separate answer.

1. When will these things be, i.e., the destruction of the Temple buildings?

2. What will be the sign of Your coming?

3. What will be the sign of the end of the age?

THE FIRST QUESTION:
THE DESTRUCTION OF JERUSALEM

Jesus began His discourse with a warning:

> Watch out that no one deceives you. For many will come in my name, claiming, "I am the Christ," and will deceive many. You will hear of wars and rumors of wars, but see to it that you are not alarmed. Such things must happen, but the end is still to come. Nation will rise against nation, and kingdom against kingdom. There will be famines and earthquakes in various places. All these are the beginning of birth pains.
>
> Then you will be handed over to be persecuted and put to death, and you will be hated by all nations because of me. At that time many will turn away from the faith and will betray and hate each other, and many false prophets will appear and deceive many people. Because of the increase of wickedness, the love of most will grow cold, but he who stands firm to the end will be saved. And this gospel of the kingdom will be preached in the whole world as a testimony to all nations, and then the end will come (Matthew 24:4-14).

These verses are a prelude to the rest of Jesus' message. They describe the general character of the end of the age: false messiahs, apostasy, wars, famines and earthquakes. Jesus pointed out that those things had to happen, "but the end is still to come." These catastrophes were generally thought to harbinger the end times, but Pax Romana was in effect. Hence, no wars. Religious zeal was at an all-time high with little apparent turning from the Jewish religion. In short, Jesus was telling them that the usually accepted notions of end-times signs would not suffice.

It is not until His next words that Jesus speaks of Jerusalem's fall:

> So when you see standing in the holy place "the abomination that causes desolation," spoken of through the prophet Daniel—let the reader understand—then let those who are in Judea flee to the mountains. Let no one on the roof of his house go down to take anything out of the house. Let no one in the field go back to get his cloak. How dreadful it will be in those days for pregnant women and nursing mothers! Pray that your flight will not take place in winter or on the Sabbath. For then there will be great distress, unequaled from the beginning of the world until now—and never to be equaled again. If those days had not been cut short, no one would survive, but for the sake of the elect those days will be shortened (Matthew 24:15-22).

It is evident in its context that this had to speak to Jewish people who would believe in Jesus. Fleeing to the hills was not exactly to be a worldwide phenomena. The Sabbath wouldn't pose a problem to Gentiles. Non-Jews were never allowed in the Temple in Jerusalem where they could see what would be the "abomination of desolation."

It is important to see that these signs most literally pertain to Jewish people living in the land. They will be the first to be able to recognize the times by the events which are happening. One thing that strikes the reader is the phrase concerning the "abomination of desolation" standing in the "holy place." Sounds mysterious, doesn't it? But to a first-century Jewish reader the meaning would be clear: The phrase "abomination of desolation" is drawn from the writings of Daniel (9:27; 11:31; 12:11) and refers to the erection of an image in the Temple complex. The Jewish prophets bitterly condemned the raising of images or idols for the purpose of worship. The people of Israel regarded idolatry as the worst sin; they abhorred it to the point where Jews didn't even make pictures or sculpt art at this time in history.

Nothing on earth was more holy, more awesome than the Temple. The abomination of desolation, the worst possible thing that could happen in the worst possible place, would stand as the ultimate insult to the God of Abraham, Isaac and Jacob. The defilement brought about by an idol in the Temple would leave the house of worship desolate of God's presence.

When does all this take place? Some see the destruction of the Temple in 70 C.E. as the fulfillment—but that presents a serious problem. If that were the time foretold, why was there no idol in the Holy Place then? Others see the very end of the age when the Temple will be rebuilt and once again defiled. Could it be that the destruction in 70 C.E. was a mere token of the destruction yet to come? Just as Saddam Hussein manifests the spirit of Antichrist, but is not himself the great, final Antichrist, could the first-century destruction of the Temple be a harbinger of later events?

Certainly at the end of the age the man of lawlessness will arise, the event that Paul referred to in the Thessalonian prophecy discussed in the last chapter. This man of lawlessness will manipulate world affairs so that he is allowed on the Temple Mount where he will set up a statue of himself in the Temple precincts. Not only is this an abomination according to the Bible, but according to rabbinic law, the Holy of Holies—the innermost and most sacred part of the Temple—exists as a zone on the Temple Mount, even in the absence of the Temple itself. That is why religious Jews do not set foot on the Temple Mount; they might inadvertently enter the Holy of Holies, where the Lord prohibited all but the high priest from entering. Today there are warning signs posted at the entrances to the Temple Mount area telling of this prohibition.

Another striking thing in the passage in Daniel is the phrase "son of man." This was a title Jesus used in reference to Himself, which He also drew from the prophet Daniel who prophesied a coming ruler:

> In my vision at night I looked, and there before me was one like a son of man, coming with the clouds of heaven. He approached the Ancient of Days and was led into his presence. He was given authority, glory and sovereign power; all peoples, nations and men of every language worshiped him. His dominion is an everlasting dominion that will not pass away, and his kingdom is one that will never be destroyed (Daniel 7:13,14).

So when Jesus speaks of the "sign of the Son of Man," he is speaking of His own return to culminate the kingdom.

QUESTION TWO:
THE SIGN OF JESUS' COMING

At that time if anyone says to you, "Look, here is the Christ!" or, "There he is!" do not believe it. For false Christs and false prophets will appear and perform great signs and miracles to deceive even the elect—if that were possible. See, I have told you ahead of time.

So if anyone tells you, "There he is, out in the desert," do not go out; or, "Here he is, in the inner rooms," do not believe it. For as lightning that comes from the east is visible even in the west, so will be the coming of the Son of Man. Wherever there is a carcass, there the vultures will gather.

Immediately after the distress of those days

> "the sun will be darkened,
> and the moon will not give its light;
> the stars will fall from the sky,
> and the heavenly bodies will be shaken."

At that time the sign of the Son of Man will appear in the sky, and all the nations of the earth will mourn. They will see the Son of Man coming on the clouds of the sky, with power and great glory. And he will send his angels with a loud trumpet call, and they will gather his elect from the four winds, from one end of the heavens to the other (Matthew 24:23-31).

Jesus answered the disciples' second question more by way of a negative than a positive response. He warned His followers that "signs" would accompany the rise of false messiahs. But the true sign will come after the distress of the preceding events. The Greek word for *sign* also means an "ensign, standard, or banner."[1]

The false messiahs will be able to do supernatural acts which are perceived as miracles. But these false miracles are not to be taken as a sign — there will be one true sign. The exact form this sign will take will not be known until it happens, but it will be the ensign of the King Messiah. So clear will this sign be, that "all the nations of the earth will mourn." But until that time, no one should be taken in by false expectations or false messiahs.

Until now, has there ever been a time in history when all nations have mourned together at the same time? I conjecture that something will happen to make the messiahship of Y'shua so apparent, that all those who didn't believe will consider their own lives wasted up to that time and their religion wrong if they had a religion that wasn't in accord with Y'shua.

QUESTION THREE:
THE SIGN OF THE END OF THE AGE

Now learn this lesson from the fig tree: As soon as its twigs get tender and its leaves come out, you know that summer is near. Even so, when you see all these things, you know that it is near, right at the door. I tell you the truth, this generation will certainly not pass away until all these things have happened (Matthew 24:32-34).

Like we often do, Jesus' followers wanted a detailed calendar with specific dates so they might know exactly what to expect at what time.

But Jesus would not give specific dates. He even disavowed knowing the time of His own return:

No one knows about that day or hour, not even the angels in heaven, nor the Son, but only the Father (Matthew 24:36).

That's why predicting a specific date is futile. Why do you think the disciples wanted to know the time these things would occur? Perhaps for the same reason so many people today are wrapped up in predicting the future. It's human to feel that knowing the future gives us a measure of control, and control is something we want more of.

It is difficult to accept that in matters of ultimate significance, we cannot have control. Yet we do have a choice. We can choose to accept the fact that God is ultimately in control; we can trust Him and concern ourselves with acting on those things which He has revealed to us. Or we can refuse to acknowledge that God has the first and last word, in which case we trust whoever or whatever seems most acceptable to us and our own way of thinking and planning.

Jesus encouraged His followers to trust God, and to do the work of encouraging others to believe. He does not leave us in total confusion regarding the future. Though we are not given the exact day and hour of things to come, God reveals enough information to provide the understanding we need.

Jesus informed His followers that they should watch for the signs of change in the season. Just as people in His day could look at a fig tree, notice the tender sprouts, and confidently assume summer was not too far away, Jesus' followers were and are to notice signs which indicate a final change of "seasons." When we see those signs, we too can confidently assume that the new "season" is not far away.

Exactly when does summer come? At what moment is the change of the season accomplished? Despite what the calendar says, no one can tell! One can see it coming and know when it gets here, but no one can predict the precise day or hour the change actually occurs. In some years it is earlier than the calendar date; in others it is later. It has more to do with the growing season than the calendar.

That's what Jesus meant when He answered His followers' question. The forces which the prophets predicted are at work. We can see the tender shoots ready to sprout. We just don't know exactly when it will happen.

We can know that when it does happen, when the forces climax, when Jesus actually does return, physically, to this earth, it will be blindingly apparent to everyone!

TWO RESPONSES

The prophets also predicted the responses which various groups of people would make when the Messiah returns. Two groups of people are spoken of in different parts of the Scripture: (1) those who have chosen to follow Jesus, including both Jews and Gentiles; and (2) those who have made a choice not to follow Him, again, both Jews and

Gentiles. Those who have chosen to follow Jesus, whether Jewish or Gentile, will have a cosmic celebration:

> Then I heard what sounded like a great multitude, like the roar of rushing waters and like loud peals of thunder, shouting:
> > "Hallelujah!
> > For the Lord God Almighty reigns.
> > Let us rejoice and be glad and give him glory!
> > (Revelation 19:6,7)

Conversely, those who have not believed in Jesus will have a different reaction. At the time the Messiah returns, there will be great sorrow and repentance.

> And I will pour out on the house of David and the inhabitants of Jerusalem a spirit of grace and supplication. They will look on me, the one they have pierced, and mourn for him as one mourns for an only child, and grieve bitterly for him as one grieves for a firstborn son. On that day the weeping in Jerusalem will be great, like the weeping of Hadad Rimmon in the plain of Megiddo. (Zechariah 12:10,11)

Zechariah revealed that the Jewish people will weep when they look upon "me, the one they have pierced." The rabbis who compiled the Talmud understood this verse to be a reference to the Messiah. Interestingly, they developed the idea that there would be two Messiahs, one of whom would suffer and die (Messiah ben Joseph) and one who would be a triumphant king (Messiah ben David). For whatever reasons, they could not accept two comings of one Messiah. Yet they had this to say about the Zechariah passage quoted above:

> What is the cause of the mourning [of Zechariah 12:12]? . . . It is well according to him who explains that the cause is the slaying of Messiah the son of Joseph, since that well agrees with the Scriptural verse, And they shall look upon me because they have thrust him

through, and they shall mourn for him as one mourneth for his ony son [Zechariah 12:10] (Babylonian Talmud (Soncino edition), Sukkah 52*a*).

Though the translation in the Talmud is a little different, the meaning is the same. Zechariah is speaking of the suffering and piercing of the Messiah, whom later history showed to be the same one who was pierced both when He was nailed to a Roman cross and when He was later pierced with a soldier's spear:

> But when they came to Jesus and found that he was already dead, they did not break his legs. Instead, one of the soldiers pierced Jesus' side with a spear, bringing a sudden flow of blood and water. The man who saw it has given testimony, and his testimony is true. He knows that he tells the truth, and he testifies so that you also may believe. These things happened so that the scripture would be fulfilled: "Not one of his bones will be broken," and, as another scripture says, "They will look on the one they have pierced" (John 19:33-37).

Zechariah's prediction was made 600 years before the crucifixion of Jesus!

It is also important to see that it is God who is saying "They shall look upon me whom they have pierced." It is important to ask, "How could God be pierced?" Is it possible that in some way the Messiah could be God?

For those of the house of Israel who have chosen not to trust in Jesus, God's Messiah, there will be tremendous grief upon realizing that Jesus, who was despised and rejected, actually was who He claimed to be. When my people think of His atoning death, it will be with the same pain and remorse that a parent would feel over the death of an only child.

But it also will be the grief of repentance and cleansing:

"On that day a fountain will be opened to the house
of David and the inhabitants of Jerusalem, to cleanse
them from sin and impurity. On that day, I will banish
the names of the idols from the land, and they will be
remembered no more," declares the LORD Almighty. "I
will remove both the prophets and the spirit of impurity
from the land" (Zechariah 13:1-2).

And if Jewish people respond in that way, what of the
response of unbelieving Gentiles? Zechariah spoke of the
grief of Israel, but Jesus also speaks of the grief of unbelieving Gentiles: "All the nations of the earth will mourn"
(Matthew 24:30).

Why should that be? If you remember what was said
in previous chapters concerning the nations gathering
against Israel in the last days, you can understand why
there will be grief at the return of the Messiah.

Then the LORD will go out and fight against those
nations, as he fights in the day of battle. On that day his
feet will stand on the Mount of Olives, east of Jerusalem,
and the Mount of Olives will be split in two from east to
west, forming a great valley, with half of the mountain
moving north and half moving south. . . . The LORD will
be king over the whole earth. On that day there will be
one LORD, and his name the only name (Zechariah 14:3,
4,9).

The book of Revelation in the New Testament also
describes the worldwide defeat of the nations:

Then I saw the beast [Antichrist, the man of law-
lessness] and the kings of the earth and their armies
gathered together to make war against the rider on the
horse [the returning Messiah] and his army. But the
beast was captured. . . . [and] the rest of them were killed
with the sword that came out of the mouth of the rider
on the horse [His words], and the birds gorged themselves on their flesh. (Revelation 19:19-21).

Is it any wonder the Jewish people will grieve in repentance over not accepting the Messiah even while God remains gracious by giving them victory over the foreign nations about them? Is it any wonder that the nations will mourn as well, as divine judgment overtakes them in the end?

THE UNASKED QUESTION

After Jesus answered His disciples' questions, He addressed a more important issue which they had not asked about: What difference should our thinking about the return of Messiah make in how we live our lives every day?

Answering that unasked question was so important to Jesus that He gave the same response in four different ways, using four different illustrations. What response was that? In a phrase: BE PREPARED! His responses deal with being prepared in light of the suddenness of His return and the fact that we should do whatever we need to do now to anticipate it.

Illustration 1. Jesus referred to the days of Noah when the great flood came in all its destructive force and caught many off guard. They perished in the destruction, because they did not take seriously the impending judgment. They were not prepared.

> As it was in the days of Noah, so it will be at the coming of the Son of Man. For in the days before the flood, people were eating and drinking, marrying and giving in marriage, up to the day Noah entered the ark; and they knew nothing about what would happen until the flood came and took them all away. That is how it will be at the coming of the Son of Man (Matthew 24:37-39).

Illustration 2. Jesus compared the moment of His coming to that of a thief who breaks into a house at night: Both are unexpected, and neither can be met appropriately unless a vigilant watch is kept all the time.

Therefore keep watch, because you do not know on what day your Lord will come. But understand this: If the owner of the house had known at what time of night the thief was coming, he would have kept watch and would not have let his house be broken into. So you also must be ready, because the Son of Man will come at an hour when you do not expect him (Matthew 24:42-44).

Illustration 3. Jesus used the example of a servant who is put in charge of the household during his master's lengthy absence. He compares the response of a trustworthy servant to that of a wicked servant who thinks the master will never find out, and is quite unprepared for his return.

Who then is the faithful and wise servant, whom the master has put in charge of the servants in his household to give them their food at the proper time? It will be good for that servant whose master finds him doing so when he returns. I tell you the truth, he will put him in charge of all his possessions. But suppose that servant is wicked and says to himself, "My master is staying away a long time," and he then begins to beat his fellow servants and to eat and drink with drunkards. The master of that servant will come on a day when he does not expect him and at an hour he is not aware of. He will cut him to pieces and assign him a place with the hypocrites, where there will be weeping and gnashing of teeth (Matthew 24:45-51).

Illustration 4. Jesus told a story about ten young women, attendants at a wedding. It is said that, in that culture, instead of going on a honeymoon, the bride and groom stayed home for a fabulous week of feasting. Part of the ritual was the bridegroom's attempt to catch the wedding party off guard. At any time of the day or night, he could come to the house where his bride had been taken. All that was required of him was that he send a runner ahead in the streets, announcing, "The bridegroom is coming." Everyone who could get ready quickly enough to enter the house with the groom was allowed to enjoy the entire week of feasting. The others were left in the cold.

In that context, Jesus' parable relates that five of the young women were wise enough to be prepared while the others were not and were left out. No preparation, no celebration!

> At that time the kingdom of heaven will be like ten virgins who took their lamps and went out to meet the bridegroom. Five of them were foolish and five were wise. The foolish ones took their lamps but did not take any oil with them. The wise, however, took oil in jars along with their lamps. The bridegroom was a long time in coming, and they all became drowsy and fell asleep.
>
> At midnight the cry rang out: "Here's the bridegroom! Come out to meet him!"
>
> Then all the virgins woke up and trimmed their lamps. The foolish ones said to the wise, "Give us some of your oil; our lamps are going out."
>
> "No," they replied, "there may not be enough for both us and you. Instead, go to those who sell oil and buy some for yourselves."
>
> But while they were on their way to buy the oil, the bridegroom arrived. The virgins who were ready went in with him to the wedding banquet. And the door was shut.
>
> Later the others also came. "Sir! Sir!" they said. "Open the door for us!"
>
> But he replied, "I tell you the truth, I don't know you."
>
> Therefore keep watch, because you do not know the day or the hour (Matthew 25:1-13).

The unasked question remains: How does one prepare?

*Will you be able to look into His face
and say, "I had no way of knowing"?*

14. BE PREPARED!

HOW NOT TO BE PREPARED

The sharp reality of our immediate circumstances can make the somewhat blurry future seem unimportant. All you have to do to be unprepared for the days ahead is tell yourself, "I'll deal with it when the time comes." The temptation to procrastinate is strong. Is there something which seems to be urging you, "Don't think about it now. It is only those things which are pressing in at the moment that are truly real"?

If you want to be unprepared, all you have to do is listen to and obey those urgings. But if you have a sense that there is something more than the material world, you might also have realized the time to deal with that "something more" and prepare for its ramifications is now, because none of us can know how much time we have.

On the opening page of this book I presented a hypothetical situation. A person who has never seen or read about African wildlife looks out the window one morning and sees a row of giraffes nibbling at the treetops lining his street. The average person will blink, look again, close the blinds and decide he didn't see what he saw. For most people, any reality which cannot be catalogued within the files of our normal experience or does not match what we feel are acceptable expectations is rejected or regarded as an aberration. But wishing won't make it so. Whatever is out there is real, whether we choose to close the blinds or not.

SOONER OR LATER THE BLINDS WILL BE LIFTED

In fact, not only will the blinds be lifted, but the walls of our house will fall down and we will be standing face to face with realities that are outside what we know and regard as safe. All of us have to face these realities when we die; some of us may have to face them during our earthly lifetime because the spiritual forces at work in this world will not wait outside forever. This can be a terrifying experience, and it will be—for those who have not chosen of their own free will to deal with spiritual realities. But it does not have to be.

WINDOWS OF PROPHECY

If there is one thing you can know from prophecy, it is that God is not some disinterested being who is content to watch us from a distance. Nor is God satisfied for you to contemplate Him from a distance. He wants a personal relationship with you!

You can know God is real and personal by gazing through windows of prophecy in the Bible. Through those windows you can see what God predicted about world events long before they happened. You can read those predictions which have been fulfilled in their entirety, such as the destruction of Tyre. You can see those predictions which have been fulfilled in part, such as the Messiah's dual role. You can see the first part fulfilled in the birth and suffering of Y'shua, Jesus, as our sin-bearer. As you see other pieces of last-day prophecies falling into place today, such as the nations gathering against Israel, you can know that what the prophecies say about the return of Jesus in the last days is also true. Through prophecy, you can know that God is not some vague, far-removed amorphous energy, but that He is very much involved with events in this world. You can know that God cares for you and wants you to share in the victory when He passes judgment on the evil that seems to dominate the world today.

The first step to being prepared is to accept the reality of spiritual forces around us.

CREATURES OUT OF CONTROL

The second step to being prepared is to realize that we are not in control of our individual or collective destinies. Take a good long look at the escalating current events viz-à-viz prophecy. It should be enough to make one realize that human beings are not in control, as individuals or as a race. Yes, we still have the ability to make certain choices—but our choices are far outweighed by the circumstances and the choices of other people who are also vying for control. The reason we are unable to control what occurs in the material world is that we are not in control of unseen forces in and around us.

Bitterness, hatred and mistrust do not start on a national level but within the hearts of individuals. How can we can stop ourselves from being sucked into a vortex of world war when we cannot stop ourselves from being sucked into the vortex of spiritual emptiness?

Have you ever wondered how so many people can be so frightened in a world as advanced as ours? Look at all the wonderful inventions and medical discoveries we've made. Look at the potential for sharing resources and ending world hunger. We know now what causes pollution and we have the knowledge to put a stop to it. And if everyone in the world would refuse to take more than what we need of anything, there would be enough of everything to go around.

Why have we not solved our problems and created a utopia?

Why must parents go into a panic if their child is out of sight for two minutes in a department store? Why is child abuse so rampant? Why is it that in most cities people lock their doors at night as a matter of common sense? Why are new strains of diseases wiping out thousands of people as soon as we find cures for the old ones? Why, when most people just want to be left in peace, are we constantly hurtling toward war?

I propose that the reason the world is out of control is that the human race is undergoing an identity crisis. I propose that as creatures who do not recognize that we were designed to glorify our creator, we have lost control of ourselves and our planet. Many people will react to that proposition with disgust, thinking God could never be so self-centered as to create a world for the purpose of glorifying Himself. Yet that very abhorrence to the idea of self-centeredness is the remnant of our true identity.

Deep inside, most of us know that it is wrong for any person to expect the world to revolve around him or her. We may unconsciously act as though we are the center of the universe by being thoughtless, careless or just plain selfish. But only a psychopath is devoid of the realization that the world does not revolve around the gratification of his or her desires.

Many people transfer this innate abhorrence of self-centeredness to God. Who is God, that He created a whole universe to revolve around Himself?

The irony is that we abhor self-centeredness because somewhere in our soul is a trace of the knowledge that no one but God is the center of the universe. God has every reason to be self-centered. Here is why: God loves what is good—and He is the source of all that is good. God loves beauty—and He is the source of all that is truly beautiful. God loves creativity—and He is the creator. God loves consistency, dependability, faithfulness, mercy, justice, righteousness, truth, wisdom and humor. God enjoys all these things—and since He is the source and perfection of all these things, is it any wonder that God loves Himself and wants all of creation to love Him also? God not only loves Himself, but He also enjoys Himself.

His own perfections are a source of tremendous cosmic joy, and He wants us to enjoy Him, too. He made us with the capacity of enjoying all of His perfections. It is only when God is central in our lives that we can be fully human and share the joy God meant us to have. Deny it though we may, if we are not God-centered, we are anthropomorphizing, man-centered and most tragically, self-centered. No matter how hard we might try, because we insist on doing things our own way, we are a race that is destroying faster than we can build. We are creatures out of control, but we can become prepared for the last days by realizing that we do not have control over those things of ultimate consequence, and by taking the next logical step.

SO GET OUT THE WINDEX

If we recognize that we are not in control, the next step is deciding whom we will trust before the crisis comes—be it the last days of the world or just the last days of our individual lives. Remember, though this world is out of control, God is not. We can be prepared for anything if we belong to Him. If we are committed to trusting God, we need to be open to what He has to say to us about who He is and what He expects. That means getting out the spiritual "Windex" and removing some of the grime of prejudice from those windowpanes of prophecy. It means looking at what the Bible has to say with open eyes and an open heart, wanting to hear what God is saying through the Scriptures.

Maybe you don't believe the Bible is God's way of revealing Himself. Would you want to know if it is? Would you be willing to read it with the understanding that you might actually meet God somewhere between the pages of Genesis and Revelation? If you apply a bit of prayer to the Scriptures before reading them and tell the Lord that you want to see whatever He wants you to see, you might be surprised at the resulting clarity of spiritual truths.

On the other hand, those who never cared to look or ask God if there was something He wanted them to see will also be surprised. When the Messiah Jesus returns, many people will hear these chilling words from His lips: "Depart from me, you who are cursed, into the eternal fire prepared for the devil and his angels."

If Jesus truly is the Messiah, will you be able to look into His face and say, "I had no way of knowing"? Are you willing to find out if He is the Messiah? Are you prepared?

15. THE FINAL CHAPTER

Some ask, "Will God's judgment and wrath be pronounced because people chose not to believe in Jesus?" The answer is a resounding, no! No! NO! The idea that what one does or doesn't believe brings judgment is nonsense. The problem lies within our own hearts, not our minds. Many people don't believe in sin, but not believing it does not make it cease to exist. In fact, sin is like AIDS of the soul—a mutating disease which breaks down our spiritual resistance, making it impossible for us to fight off the simplest bacteria. We are overcome by the most ordinary temptations to obey our own inclinations rather than believe and obey God. The tiniest bit of the sin virus is deadly.

And we all have it.

THE NAZI REFUSED

In the beginning of World War II, hostilities broke out in the North Sea. A German merchant vessel carrying a Nazi military crew was shelled by British warships. After two direct hits, the merchant vessel slowly began sinking into the wintry cold North Sea.

The crew abandoned ship, plunging into the icy waters. British lifeboats rushed to rescue the survivors.

One lifeboat came upon a lone German seaman, struggling to stay afloat as he convulsed with the cold. A British man reached over the side of the lifeboat and extended his hand to pull his enemy to safety.

The Nazi looked up, his face already tinted with a bluish cast, and he spat at the face of the British seaman whose hand was outstretched. He turned, and with the energy that remained in his rapidly chilling body, swam away to certain death in the frigid black water.

Did he drown because the man in the lifeboat didn't save him?

Did he drown because he spat in the sailor's face and swam away?

NO! He drowned because he was in a cold sea that couldn't sustain life.

We live and move in a matrix of sin that cannot sustain our spiritual life. It is only a matter of time until we sink into the cold reality of our alienation from God. Those who are spiritually alert recognize that there is a growing crisis. They can see that we are stumbling in a darkness so thick we can't even see the ticking clock to know whether it is just before midnight or five o'clock in the morning.

All we know is that it has been dark for a long time.

The prophesied Messiah has come, and He is returning soon. He is like the sailor with his hand extended:

> You see, at just the right time, when we were still powerless, Christ [Messiah] died for the ungodly. Very rarely will anyone die for a righteous man, though for a good man someone might possibly dare to die. But God demonstrates his own love for us in this: While we were still sinners, Christ [Messiah] died for us (Romans 5:6-8).

ACCEPTING THE UNACCEPTABLE

This good news, the "gospel," is an offense to many, so many reject it. Some reject the idea that they are sinners. Others are appalled by the idea that God actually required death, someone's blood, to pay for people's sins. To still others, the cross and what it has represented throughout history is reprehensible.

I was 17 and it was Yom Kippur, the Day of Atonement, when I first heard the news about Jesus dying for me. That day I happened to be by myself, waiting on Larimer Street in Denver, Colorado, for the number 61 bus. A young man named Orville struck up a conversation with me and began to talk to me about the prophecy of the Bible and the last days.

It was 1949. Israel had been a state for only a matter of months. Orville told me the Bible prophesied that the Jewish people would return to our ancient homeland. He said that God loved the Jewish people and, according to the Hebrew prophets, He still had plans for our future as a nation. To hear a Gentile talk about my own religion in a positive, respectful way impressed me.

When he began to tell me about Jesus, a bell went off in my mind, "Warning! Warning! Unacceptable religion!" I immediately knew I would not believe a word he said because to believe in Jesus would mean rejecting my Jewishness and embracing a Gentile religion (or so I thought at the time). My filter was switched on and I was prepared to listen politely and disregard whatever came next.

The first thing he pointed out was that all people have sinned and none of us measure up to God's standard. Despite my resolve not to believe anything he said, his statement that everyone has sinned came as good news to me. Though I'd never thought about it much, I realized deep down that, if there was a God, I must have offended Him. It hadn't occurred to me that anyone else had the same problem.

Further, when I heard Orville explain about sin and its alienating effect, it was as though he had explained myself to me! At last it was clear why, in spite of my ideals, I wasn't able to do what I wanted to do, and why, in spite of my disgust, I had an underlying perversity in my nature.

Many people don't accept the gospel as good news because to them it begins with an insult: "All have sinned!" I accepted what others deemed unacceptable—with regard to the fact that God was not pleased with me.

The second part of the gospel is an even bigger insult: "Christ died for our sins according to the Scripture."

Who asked Him to?

I recognized my sin but the solution was too much. I didn't want to be that deeply obligated to anyone for anything. I'd rather do it for myself, thank you.

Yet there was something else I knew about myself. Deep down I knew I was helpless to live up to my ideals. It was not that I never behaved decently. I just knew that many times I had tried to do what I understood was the right thing and had failed. I just couldn't do it for myself. I had never heard that someone else could and would do it for me.

I was only 17 years old.

I didn't exactly believe it. I was skeptical, especially about the resurrection. Still, even though I had not accepted it, I was worried because what Orville said seemed to make sense. I was certain that the rabbis could pick this guy's argument to pieces. Why couldn't I?

I decided that the only reason it made any sense to me was that I was dumb. What this guy had said was too good. Not too complicated, just too good. And too simple. I had always thought religion was mysterious, and much too complicated to be understood unless you had studied it for years. Maybe if Orville had told me something more exotic—a learned path, a formula which required a multitude of difficult steps to follow, or something mysterious—it might have had more credibility.

Some years back there was a commercial on television—I can't remember the product, but I can remember the tone of voice of the young woman who said, "Mother, please! I'd rather do it myself!"

The tone was poignant, demanding, insistent, impatient, angry and most of all, assertive. If you ever heard that commercial, you know which one I mean.

Somehow we tend to think those things we do are better than the things done for us . . . the things we earn are better than the things given. The things we choose to use are better than the procedures others present to us. At least by exercising the will, we feel stronger and we have a better sense of self. I believe this is one of the many reasons for the new religions which continually rise on the scene. Sometimes the more obtuse or weird the religion, the more wonderful it seems to the self-willed, self-centered person. People who laugh at the idea of someone dying for their sins and rising from the dead can, on the other hand, without the slightest bit of scientific evidence, believe that some good comes about by holding crystals in a particular way.

Over the next four years, it dawned on me that one of my basic assumptions about life was dead wrong: Human beings don't start out good and then turn bad, as I had believed. They start out bent and they end up broken and there is no splint within a person's heart that can straighten it out.

Then I had a breakthrough. It happened when I was explaining to my wife why I didn't believe that some radio preacher's idea of heaven was right. I suddenly realized that the reason I believed his idea was wrong was that I had another idea, a belief which I hadn't even been aware of, much less articulated.

Eternal life is not something that begins after we die. It's something that always has been. That's why it is eternal. We are not eternal, but are born into this stream of true God-consciousness that always has existed. All those who ever strove for eternal life were wrong. It's always there, but it is unreachable from our position as sinful creatures in a sinful world.

God makes it clear that the wages of sin is death, which is separation from God. Yet God loved each one of us so much that He allowed Jesus to suffer death on the cross to pay for our sin. Through that death in our place He has made it possible for you and me to enter into eternal life. When we repent of the sin that separates us from God, and we accept Jesus' life-giving sacrifice on the cross as full payment for our sin, we gain God's forgiveness and are born into that eternal life.

We don't have to learn secret knowledge; we don't have to torture ourselves; we don't have to meditate ourselves up the ladder of consciousness. In fact, none of those things can help us.

We just have to know one thing: Y'shua Ha'Mashiach, Jesus the Messiah, is the promised Redeemer for Jews and Gentiles.

EYES ON THE HORIZON –
THE DAWN IS NEARING

The sure word of prophecy in the Scripture promises that the dawn is nearing. Look around you and see if our world is the one that prophecy describes. Listen closely as the orchestra begins. Can you hear the themes? The piece they are playing is "The Overture to Armageddon."

If we will look up we can see the horizon and the promise of the dawn. Through the Scriptures we can see the One who died for our sins, reaching His hand out toward us to lift us from the icy gloom. If you are prepared to accept that hand, you can be lifted into a new life right now.

First, you must admit that your sin has separated you from God. Read the words of the ancient Jewish prophet Isaiah:

> But your iniquities have separated
>   you from your God;
> your sins have hidden his face from you,
>   so that he will not hear (Isaiah 59:2).

Next, you need to recognize that God is waiting and wanting to forgive you and bring you out of the darkness of sin into His wonderful light. He wants to hear your words of repentance.

The Bible says:

> If we confess our sins, he is faithful and just and will forgive us our sins and purify us from all unrighteousness (1 John 1:9).

and also,

> If you confess with your mouth, "Jesus is Lord," and believe in your heart that God raised him from the dead, you will be saved (Romans 10:9).

Whether you are Jewish or Gentile, by accepting that Jesus is your Messiah and Lord, you can know that . . .

> You are a chosen people, a royal priesthood, a holy nation, a people belonging to God, that you may declare the praises of him who called you out of darkness into his wonderful light (1 Peter 2:9).

You can claim these promises from God's Word. You can enter into a personal relationship with your creator by making a commitment with this simple prayer:

"God, I know that what the prophets have said is true of me as well. I know that I am not what I should be and that by breaching Your standards I have separated myself from You. I do believe the promises in the Bible and I do believe that Jesus came and paid the price for my sin. I believe that He was raised from the dead and that by trusting and giving my life to Him, I will have a relationship with You and life everlasting. Thank You, in the name of Jesus, the Messiah. Amen."

Have you just prayed that prayer? If you have done so for the very first time, would you drop us a quick note to let us know? We'd like to tell you a hearty *mazel tov* and rejoice with you! Write to . . .

Jews for Jesus
60 Haight Street
San Francisco, CA 94102

MEANWHILE, BACK AT THE TEACHERS' LOUNGE

" ... yes, we're all educated people, but we're not educated enough until we read the Word of God," Lovelle finished. She sat back and smiled.

The ringing of the class bell broke the silence.

"Whew!" Sam exhaled. "Saved, so to speak, by the bell . . . and boys' basketball!" He jumped up and darted for the door, slam-dunking his empty Diet Coke can into the trash on his way out. Sam's wry smile hid the discomfort that had mounted inside him with all this talk of Jesus. He couldn't put his finger on it, but something just didn't feel right.

Evelyn stood to gather her papers. "Well, Lovelle, I respect your straightforwardness. I'm not sure I agree, but I have to say this is all, well, very interesting. But right now I really need to prepare for my next class."

That left Lovelle and Tessie. "How about you, Tessie?" Lovelle asked softly. "Are you prepared?"

*　　*　　*

An Afterword . . .

THE RETURN

So the orb on which we live might not be able to sustain life much longer. The malady of man is sin. The earth which should have been cultivated by man, preserved by man and made to show forth the glory of God is showing only how thoughtless, wasteful, selfish and violent is the human species.

Ecologically speaking, the sin cancer has metasticized throughout the whole earth and the planet is a terminal case. Not only is the ground that we stand on sick, but human character also has shown itself to be of such a nature that improvements do not lead to peace. More education shows us how to make better weapons. In modern days, the electronic marvels of communication seem to have brought us back to trying to rebuild the Tower of Babel whereby we show our own greatness and try to block out the vision of God.

Mankind's possibilities for peace are disappearing daily and continued conflict seems inevitable. Those who want moral government are legislatively tied up whereas those who respect no law have all the modern advantages, and the city streets become jungles. The axiomatic truth of evolution which calls for the survival of the fittest must be modified to now explain survival in terms of violence capabilities. The Golden Rule, as we so aptly put it, has become "he who has the gold rules." And the whole world is now looking for something, someone to solve the insolvable problems.

There is a growing clamor from the edges of each society asking for a peacemaker, life-giver, provider—and soon that clamor will be worldwide, asking for a man to do for us what only God should do.

Such a man will be presented.

His name might be Saddam Hussein or another name, but he will talk about peace. He will talk about brotherhood. He will talk about prosperity and seem to have the strength to bring it about. He will explain his killings of people as being necessary for the good of all. He will offer the atrocities that he performs as tokens of his love for humanity, saying that he loves his fellow man so much that he had to take this drastic action on our behalf. Others will begin to speak of him as a savior and some will call him a god and he will modestly step aside, not ready to claim those titles for himself but allowing them to be bestowed by sycophantic followers.

Times are bad. They're getting worse. The world scene is being set for that pseudo-savior who will certainly come. He will promise, then cheat; offer, then hold back; speak of life, and commit unspeakable brutalities upon the many he will slaughter. He will be a Hitler, a Haman, a Hussein, with the same demon force that filled the Marquis de Sade. He will glory in his ability to cause pain to others! He will exult in the destruction that he can cause! Then—

The one who can truly save will appear on the scene!

HOW SHOULD WE THEN LIVE?

What we believe about Y'shua's return will determine much of the way we live. The Scripture says it is the blessed hope, and if indeed it is, we're to hope for little in this world. If we truly anticipate living in a heavenly mansion, we will not seek to build mansions for ourselves here below. If we believe Y'shua truly is coming to set up His kingdom, we will not build little religious empires here on earth.

Dr. Charles Anderson, founder of Northeastern Bible College, in addressing the students, held up a half dollar in chapel. He said, "Your life is like a coin. You can spend it any way you like, but you can spend it only once." If we make our hope to be the coming of our Messiah, and if we live in the light of that blessed hope, we'll not be satisfied with the music of the moment here on earth. We'll be looking forward to the concert of the infinite multitude of harmonies where every soul will unite in a new song. Creation will be a resting point on the way to the "great rest" of the whole re-creation.

The good news for humanity is not merely that Jesus died for our sins according to the Scripture, and was buried and rose from the dead (1 Corinthians 15:3). The continuing good news is that He's also coming back soon. There are many date-setters who look into the newspaper instead of the Bible for signs of the times. No doubt before the end of this millennium, there will be many, even with Ph.D.s, who will talk about the Lord coming in the year 2000. Such is the deceitful and deceived heart, and the wishful thinkers are easily misled. But according to the Word of God, we are to hold our hearts in readiness and live each day as if the Lord is keeping His appointment with destiny tomorrow.

Ask me. Just ask me when Jesus is coming, and I'll tell you He might well come tomorrow morning!

Appendix A

SOME RABBINIC VIEWS ON THE COMING OF THE MESSIAH

The following is a selection of views held in various Jewish circles from the days of early rabbinic literature until the present.

These quotations reveal the variety of understanding in what the messianic hope consists of and gives us much insight into the thinking of our Jewish people over the centuries. Yet in the face of such divergent views, how much better it is to rely on the "sure word of prophecy" found in the Scriptures.

● The Babylonian Talmud (Soncino ed.), Sanhedrin 97*a-b*, compiled 6th-7th c. C.E.:

The Tanna debe Eliyyahu teaches: The world is to exist six thousand years. In the first two thousand years there was desolation; two thousand years the Torah flourished; and the next two thousand years is the Messianic era, but through our many iniquities all these years have been lost.

The Soncino edition footnotes this last sentence as follows: "He should have come at the beginning of the last two thousand years; the delay is due to our sins."

● The Babylonian Talmud (Soncino ed.), Sanhedrin 99*a*, compiled 6th-7th c. C.E.:

R. Hillel said: There shall be no Messiah for Israel, because they have already enjoyed him in the days of Hezekiah.

R. Joseph said: May God forgive him [for saying so].

Now, when did Hezekiah flourish? During the first Temple. Yet Zechariah, prophesying in the days of the second, proclaimed, "Rejoice greatly, O Daughter of Zion; shout, O Daughter of Jerusalem! See, your king comes to you, righteous and having salvation, gentle and riding on a donkey, on a colt, the foal of a donkey" (Zechariah 9:9).

The comment in the Jewish Encyclopedia (vol. VI, p. 401) is noteworthy: "[Hillel] may have been prompted to this declaration by Origen's [a Christian theologian of the 3rd c. C.E.] professed discovery in the Old Testament of Messianic passages referring to the founder of Christianity."

● Leviticus Rabbah (Soncino ed.) 2.2.4, 5th-7th c. C.E.:

R. Johanan said: "Rabbi used to expound 'There shall step forth a star (kokab) out of Jacob (Num. xxiv, 17)' thus: read not 'kokab' but kozab (lie). When R. Akiba beheld Bar Koziba [also known as Bar Kochba] he exclaimed, 'This is the king Messiah!' R. Johanan b. Tortha retorted: 'Akiba, grass will grow in your cheeks and he will still not have come!'

● Pesikta Rabbati, ch. 35, 9th c. C.E.:

R. Yitzhaq said: "In the year in which King Messiah will be revealed, all the kings of the nations of the world will provoke each other. The king of Persia will provoke the king of Arabia, and the king of Arabia will go to Aram [Syria] to take counsel from them. And he will drive back the king of Persia and devastate the whole world, and all the nations of the world will tremble and fear and fall upon their faces. And pangs will take hold of them like unto the pangs of a woman in childbirth. And Israel will tremble and fear, and they will say: 'Where shall we come and go, where shall we come and go?'

"And He will say to them: 'My children, fear not! Everything I did, I did only for you! Why then should you be afraid? Fear not, the time of your redemption is come. And this last redemption will not be like the first redemption, for after the first redemption you suffered pain and enslavement by kingdoms, but after this last redemption you will suffer no pain nor enslavement by kingdoms.' " (p. 173)

● Saadia Gaon, 10th c. C.E.

Messiah cannot yet have come, since we see the nations actually warring and fighting as violently as possible.[1]

● Midrash Tehillim, Psalm 119, ed. Buber, pp. 488-89, 10th-11th c. C.E.:

R. Y'huda ha Levi bar Shalom, R. Pinhas haKohen, and Rav Huna all said that Gog and Magog would come against Israel in the future three times, and the third time they would come up against Jerusalem and go to Judah, and dictate to them, for they are mighty men . . .

"Behold I will make Jerusalem a cup of staggering unto all the peoples round about" (Zechariah 12:2). What is "cup of staggering"? [It means] that He will in the future make peoples drink the cup of staggering of blood. . . . When they [Gog and Magog] go up there, what do they do? They assign two warriors to every one of the Children of Israel. Why? So that they should not escape. When the heroes of Judah ascend and reach Jerusalem, they pray in their heart. . . . In that hour the Holy One, blessed be He, gives heroism to Judah and they draw their weapons and smite those men on their right and on their left, and slay them.[2]

● Maimonides, 12th c. C.E.:

The Jew, unless he wishes to forfeit his claim to eternal life by denial of his faith, must, in acceptance of the teachings of Moses and the prophets down to Malachi, believe that the Messiah will issue forth from the house of David in the person of a descendant of Solomon, the only legitimate king; and he shall far excel all rulers in history by his reign, glorious in justice and peace. Neither impatience nor deceptive calculation of the time of the advent of the Messiah should shatter this belief.

Still, notwithstanding the majesty and wisdom of the Messiah, he must be regarded as a mortal being like any other and only as the restorer of the Davidic dynasty. He will die and leave a son as his successor, who will in his turn die and leave the throne to his heir.

Nor will there be any material change in the order of things in the whole system of nature and human life; accordingly Isaiah's picture of the living together of lamb and wolf cannot be taken literally, nor any of the Haggadic sayings with reference to the Messianic time.

We are only to believe in the coming of Elijah as a messenger of peace and the forerunner of the Messiah, and also in the great decisive battle with the hosts of heathendom embodied in Gog and Magog, through whose defeat the dominion of the Messiah will be permanently established. . . .

The Messianic kingdom itself is to bring the Jewish nation its political independence, but not the subjection of all the heathen nations, nor merely material prosperity and sensual pleasure, but an era of general affluence and peace, enabling the Jewish people to devote their lives without care or anxiety to the study of the Torah and universal wisdom, so that by their teachings they may lead all mankind to the knowledge of God and make them also share in the eternal bliss of the world to come.[3]

All these matters concerning Messiah's advent will not be known to anyone until they happen.[4]

● The Pittsburgh Platform, founding document of American Reform Judaism, 1885 C.E.:

We recognize in the modern era of universal culture of heart and intellect the approach of the realization of Israel's great Messianic hope for the establishment of the kingdom of truth, justice and peace among all men. We consider ourselves no longer a nation but a religious community, and therefore expect neither a return to Palestine, nor a sacrificial worship under the administration of the sons of Aaron, nor the restoration of any of the laws concerning the Jewish state.[5]

● Chaim Weizmann (speech to the Zionist Congress, 1937 C.E.):

   I make a sharp distinction between the present realities and the Messianic hope . . . a hope which the nation cannot forget without ceasing to be a nation. A time will come when there shall be neither enemies nor frontiers, when war shall be no more, and men will be secure in the dignity of man.[6]

● A recent news article, March 8, 1991 C.E.:

Rebbe correctly predicts war's end; is Messiah next?
By Garth Wolkoff
Of the Bulletin Staff

   The Persian Gulf war ended before Purim—just like Rabbi Menachem Schneerson said it would.

   When President Bush halted Operation Desert Storm at midnight Wednesday of last week, he made a soothsayer out of the Lubavitcher spiritual leader, who had predicted the gulf conflict would be over by the holiday.

   But the Brooklyn rebbe's prognostications didn't end when he told a U.S. military chaplain last fall not to bring his Megillah to Saudi Arabia because the war would be over by February 28. He also forecast the coming of the Messiah.

   "Moshiach will come now that the war is over. We're talking very soon," echoed Rabbi Manis Friedman, a Lubavitcher Chassidic rabbi from Minnesota who authored the recent book *Doesn't Anyone Blush Anymore?* and hosts a weekly cable-TV talk show, in an interview this week.

   The Messiah will come "before the end of the year," said Friedman, who originally had reiterated Schneerson's forecasts at a San Francisco press conference in January.

   According to Schneerson, an 1,800-year-old Jewish scholarly prophecy predicted that the Messiah would come after a war between a joint Arab-superpower force and the king of Persia—a war bearing a striking resemblance to the recent gulf clash. Schneerson and the Lubavitchers had said that in the case of this war, the king of Persia was really the leader of the Persian Gulf, Iraqi President Saddam Hussein.

After the war, a period of moral chaos should follow, the Lubavitchers quote the Midrash as saying, and then the Messiah will come.

Schneerson's prediction that the war would end before Purim, and the connection he drew between the final war illustrated in the Midrash and the Persian Gulf, "was pure inspiration," Friedman claimed. "It was the rebbe, he's the man." . . .

Although Schneerson would not consent to a telephone interview, his spokesman in Brooklyn, Rabbi Yehuda Karinsky, who says he speaks for the Lubavitcher—or Chabad—movement and not for Schneerson because "the rebbe speaks for himself," said miracles in Israel and the conclusion of the war are testimony that the Messiah will soon arrive.

Furthermore, that only two people died as a direct result of Iraq's 39 Scud missile attacks on Israel constitutes a miracle and portends Moshiach's arrival, Karinsky and Friedman agreed.

"Recent events make [the coming of the Messiah] a lot closer to reality," Karinsky said from his car phone in New York. "We never needed proof that Moshiach would come, but everybody who was informed [about the few Scud fatalities] was touched in a very real and direct way, recognizing that there were miracles."

Though Schneerson has kept mum recently about the war and his predictions, Friedman, whose rising media star could make him better known in lay circles than Schneerson, has been expounding about the rebbe and his predictions on his television show and to the press.

But Friedman has taken a little heat for so resolutely forecasting the coming of the Messiah and quoting the rebbe.

"People were saying you can't be so explicit about whether he will come," he said. "'Those who believe the Moshiach will come will believe, and those who don't won't believe. You can't put yourself on the line like that,' people told me."

What if the Messiah doesn't come?

"If it doesn't happen, don't be angry at me, be angry at him [the Messiah]," he responded to the question.

Regardless, because of the rebbe's successful Purim prediction, Friedman said he expects non-believing Jews now will take Schneerson's words a little more seriously. "With all these events, it makes believing much easier."

Israel has entered an age of untold miracles, he said, a foreshadowing of the day the Messiah heralds the downfall of the world's evil and the advent of a new moral order.

"We have entered a new world order, just like George Bush said we would, although he may not have understood himself," Friedman said . . . [7]

* * *

Appendix B

REFERENCES TO ZION, ISRAEL, AND JERUSALEM IN THE JEWISH LITURGY

● On the consecration of a house:

Bestow thy blessings upon the master of this house. Bless, O Lord, his substance, and accept the work of his hands. Keep him far from sin and transgressing. Let thy grace be upon him, and prosper thou his labours and undertakings. . . . May thy gracious promise be realised in them. Blessed shalt thou be when thou comest in, blessed when thou goest out. And even as we have been permitted to consecrate this house, so grant that we may together witness the dedication of thy great and holy temple in Jerusalem, the city of our solemnities, speedily in our days. Amen.[8]

● In the marriage ceremony:

May she who was barren (Zion) be exceeding glad and exult, when her children are gathered within her in joy. Blessed art thou, O Lord, who makest Zion joyful through her children.

O make these loved companions greatly to rejoice, even as of old thou didst gladden thy creature in the garden of Eden. Blessed art thou, O Lord, who makest bridegroom and bride to rejoice.[9]

● In the afternoon service for festivals:

Lord our God, look with favor on Thy people Israel and their prayer. Restore worship to Thy Temple in Zion, and with loving grace accept Israel's offering and prayer. May the worship of Thy people Israel find favor with Thee evermore. And may our eyes witness Thy loving return to Zion. Blessed art Thou who will restore His Divine Presence to Zion.[10]

● In the Mourner's Kaddish (prayer for the dead):

He who maketh peace in his high places, may he make peace for us and for all Israel, and say ye Amen.[11]

● Before the Torah reading in the afternoon service for Sabbath:

And it came to pass, whenever the ark started, Moses would say: "Arise, O Lord, and let thy enemies be scattered; let those who hate thee flee before thee." Truly, out of Zion shall come forth Torah, and the word of the Lord out of Jerusalem.[12]

● In the Kedushah in the morning service for Sabbath and Festivals:

From thy abode, our King, appear and reign over us, for we wait for thee. O when wilt thou reign in Zion? Speedily, in our days, do thou dwell there forever. Mayest thou be exalted and sanctified in Jerusalem thy city throughout all generations and to all eternity.[13]

● In the grace after meals:

When the Lord restored the prosperity of Zion, we were like unto them that dream. Then was our mouth filled with laughter, and our tongue with exultation: then said they among the nations, The Lord hath done great things for them.[14]

● On the Day of Atonement:

And thou, O Lord, shalt reign, thou alone over all thy works on Mount Zion, the dwelling-place of thy glory, and in Jerusalem, thy holy city, as it is written in thy Holy Words, The Lord shall reign for ever, thy God, O Zion, unto all generations. Praise ye the Lord.[15]

● When the ark is opened on Simchat Torah:

Thy kingdom is an everlasting kingdom,
And Thy dominion is through all generations.
For from Zion shall go forth Torah,
And the word of the Lord from Jerusalem.
"Father of mercy," In Thy loving will do good to Zion
And build up the walls of Jerusalem.
For our trust is in Thee alone, our divine King, God sublimely exalted,
Lord of the universe.[16]

*　　*　　*

Appendix C

GOD'S PROMISES TO ISHMAEL

God loves the Jew. He also loves the Arab. Isaiah points out that "in that day," a term often used in apocalyptic literature to refer to the last days, there will be "a sign and witness to the Lord of hosts in the land of Egypt. . . . And the Lord will make himself known to the Egyptians; and the Egyptians will know the Lord in that day" (19:20,21). Likewise, Isaiah says, "Blessed be Egypt my people, and Assyria the work of my hands, and Israel my heritage" (19:25).

Jesus said that Tyre and Sidon, the southern port cities in Lebanon, would have repented long before the cities of Bethsaida and Corazin, located in what is now Israel, and that "it shall be more tolerable on the day of judgment for Tyre and Sidon than for you" (Matthew 11:22). Tyre and Sidon are Arab cities.[17]

The following are some of the Scripture verses that specifically relate to promises God has made concerning Ishmael, and that show God's love for the Arab peoples:

The angel added, "I will so increase your descendants that they will be too numerous to count." The angel of the LORD also said to her: "You are now with child and you will have a son. You shall name him Ishmael, for the LORD has heard of your misery. He will be a wild donkey of a man; his hand will be against everyone and everyone's hand against him, and he will live in hostility toward all his brothers." She gave this name to the LORD who spoke to her: "You are the God who sees me," for she said, "I have now seen the One who sees me" (Genesis 16:10-13).

[The Lord to Abraham] "And as for Ishmael, I have heard you: I will surely bless him; I will make him fruitful and will greatly increase his numbers. He will be the father of twelve rulers, and I will make him into a great nation" (Genesis 17:20).

I will make the son of the maidservant into a nation also, because he is your offspring (Genesis 21:13).

Lift the boy up and take him by the hand, for I will make him into a great nation (Genesis 21:18).

These are the names of the sons of Ishmael, listed in the order of their birth: Nebaioth the firstborn of Ishmael, Kedar, Adbeel, Mibsam, Mishma, Dumah, Massa, Hadad, Tema, Jetur, Naphish and Kedemah. These were the sons of Ishmael, and these are the names of the twelve tribal rulers according to their settlements and camps (Genesis 25:13-16).

God's promise of descendants and a nation have been amply fulfilled in the history of the Arab peoples. Certainly Hagar saw God's love and graciousness in these promises, for God saw her and had compassion on her in her distress, and she called God, "The God who sees me."

Notes

Chapter 6

1. Barton Payne is the scholar. His book is titled, *Encyclopedia of Biblical Prophecy,* published by Baker Books, Grand Rapids, MI.
2. Historical references taken from the following: *Encyclopedia Britannica*; *History of Alexander and Indica, the Greek historian Arrian,* from the Loeb Classical Library Edition (Cambridge: Harvard University Press).

Chapter 7

1. Taken from *Evidence That Demands a Verdict* by Josh McDowell (San Bernardino, CA: Campus Crusade for Christ, 1972).
2. John N. Oswalt, "The Book of Isaiah, Chapters 1-39," *The New International Commentary on the Old Testament* (Grand Rapids, MI: Eerdmans, 1986), p. 210.
3. Bauer, *Greek-English Lexicon* (Chicago: University of Chicago Press).
4. From the introduction to *Science Speaks* (Chicago: Moody Press, 1963).
5. *Ibid,* p. 95
6. *Ibid,* pp. 96-98.

Chapter 9

1. Noah Lucas, "Zionism," *The Blackwell Companion to Jewish Culture From the 18th Century to the Present,* Glenda Abramson, ed. (Oxford, England and Cambridge, MA: Basil Blackwell Ltd. and Inc., 1989), p. 824.
2. Barnett Litvinoff, *Israel: a Chronology and Fact Book* (Dobbs Ferry, New York: Oceana Publications, 1974).
3. Lucas, *Op. Cit.*
4. Michael Kelly in *Esquire* (February 1991).
5. Quoted from Garth Wolkoff, *The Northern California Jewish Bulletin,* Volume 140, No. 5 (February 1, 1991). Used by permission.
6. P.L.O. representative Husseini, quoted in *The New York Times International Edition* (March 4, 1991).
7. Prominent Palestinian lawyer, Khalid al-Kidra, quoted in *Ibid.*

Chapter 10

1. H. A. R. Gibb, *The Arabs* (Oxford: Clarendon Press, 1940).
2. "Islam," *Time* magazine (April 16, 1979).
3. *Ibid.*
4. *Ibid.*
5. *Ibid.*
6. "Iraq," *The Encyclopedia Britannica.*
7. *Myths and Facts 1980—A Concise Record of the Arab-Israeli Conflict.* Edited by Alan M. Tigay, Near East Research, Inc., 1980.
8. *Ibid.*
9. *Ibid.*

10. *Ibid.*

11. *Ibid.*

12. Ariel Sharon in an interview with the *Los Angeles Times* (November 6, 1990).

13. Saddam Hussein quoted by the *Los Angeles Times* (October 12, 1990).

14. *USA Today,* cover story (February 8-10, 1991).

15. Quoted by *Newsweek* (February 11, 1991).

16. *Ibid.*

17. Louis Goldberg, *Turbulence Over the Middle East* (Neptune, NJ: Loizeaux Brothers, 1982).

Chapter 13

1. Carson, D. A. "Matthew" in *The Expositor's Bible Commentary* (Grand Rapids, MI: Zondervan, 1984), 8:505.

Appendices

1. Emunot VeDeot, 933, 8.8.

2. Quoted in R. Patai, *The Messiah Texts* (New York: Avon Books, 1979), p. 150.

3. Maimonides, Commentary to Sanh. X; Yad, H. Melakim, XI-XII; H. Teshubah VIII-IX; quoted in K. Kohler, *Jewish Theology Systematically and Historically Considered* (New York: Macmillan, 1918), pp. 386-87.

4. Maimonides, Yad, Melakim, 1180, 12.2 quoted in Joseph L. Baron, ed., *A Treasury of Jewish Quotations: New Revised Edition* (South Brunswick, NJ: Thomas Yoseloff, 1965), p. 306.

5. Quoted in Nicholas De Lange, *Judaism* (Oxford and New York: Oxford University Press, 1986), p. 135.

6. Quoted in Baron, *Treasury,* p. 309.

7. Garth Wolkoff, "Rebbe correctly predicts war's end; is Messiah next?" *The Northern California Jewish Bulletin* (March 8, 1991), p. 1.

8. Joseph H. Hertz, *The Authorised Daily Prayer Book: Revised Edition* (New York: Bloch Publishing Company, 1948, 1975), p. 1023.

9. *Ibid,* p. 1013.

10. *The Traditional Prayer Book for Sabbath and Festivals* (New Hyde Park, NY: University Books, Inc., 1960), p. 400.

11. Hertz, *Daily Prayer Book,* p. 555.

12. Philip Birnbaum, *Daily Prayer Book,* Ha-Siddur Ha-Shalem (New York: Hebrew Publishing Company), 1949, p. 444.

13. *Ibid,* p. 352.

14. Hertz, *Daily Prayer Book,* p. 965.

15. Hertz, *Daily Prayer Book,* p. 899.

16. *Traditional Prayer Book,* p. 572.

17. Wesley G. Pippert, *Land of Promise, Land of Strife: Israel at Forty* (Waco, TX: Word Books, 1988), p. 175.